Chocolate, Truffles

& other Treasures of Italy's

Piedmont Cuisine

© 2005 Daniela Piazza Editore
n. 13 Via Sanfront - 10138 Torino - Italia
Tel. +39 011 434.27.06 r.a. - Fax +39 011 434.24.71
www.danielapiazzaeditore.com
info@danielapiazzaeditore.com

Progetto grafico
D.P.E. Torino

Finito di stampare nel mese di dicembre 2005
presso Esperia s.r.l. - Lavis Trento

ISBN 88-7889-173-8

Chocolate, Truffles
& other Treasures of Italy's
Piedmont Cuisine

written
& illustrated by

Sally Spector

Daniela Piazza Editore

....to all those who, in one way or another, in the past and present, have contributed to growing, exchanging or producing the foods that have made it possible to write and illustrate this book. There is no way that I can personally and adequately express my deep appreciation for the help and encouragement that so many people in the Piedmont gave me: they have a special place in my thoughts and I thank them very much. A separate thanks goes to Franco, for his support, his patience and for just being there.

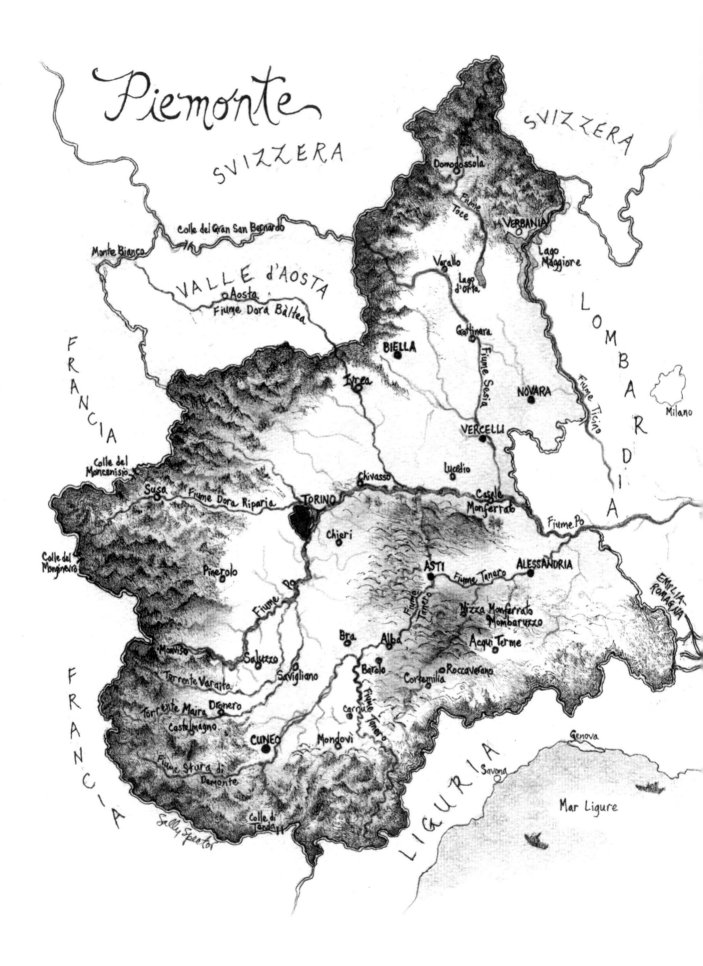

Table of Contents

Palazzo dell'Università, *Turin*

The palazzo was commissioned by the Duke of Savoy Vittorio Amedeo II: designed by the architect Michelangelo Garove, it was begun in 1712, inaugurated in 1720 & completed in the 1730's by Filippo Juvarra, Antonio Bertola & Giovanni Antonio Ricca. The square courtyard, surrounded by majestic columns & porticoes, presents a history of this institution through the numerous busts & stone plaques it contains recording eminent scholars, scientists & rulers, including one for the degree in Theology awarded to Erasmus of Rotterdam in 1506. The University, originally called LO STUDIO, was founded in 1404 but due to political events, especially France's occupation of Turin, it was occasionally closed & transferred to other cities (Chieri, Savigliano, Mondovì...). Finally, in 1566, it returned to its birthplace though studies were interrupted again in the late 1700's & the first half of the 1800's. Today, the numerous departments of the University of Turin are located in various parts of the city.

A Preliminary Note...

The recipes in this book are Italian ones, Piedmontese to be more precise, translated into English, not rewritten for, or adapted to, non-Italian kitchens. Thus, ideally, the ingredients should conform as closely as possible to those used here. One of the reasons why food in Italy is so good is because most dishes are made from fresh, not frozen or canned, local ingredients, which is why this cuisine changes so much from region to region and why it often seems virtually impossible to reproduce the flavors that one encounters here. In truth, it sometimes is impossible, for water, soil composition, sunlight... cannot be transplanted but a few "rules" will help to ensure better, more authentic results.

1) **Olive Oil** should always be ITALIAN EXTRA VIRGIN
2) **Butter**　Italian butter is never salted. If unsalted butter is not available, take into consideration the amount of salt used when cooking. Margarine is never a satisfying substitute.
3) **Vinegar**　Use only WINE, never Balsamic, VINEGAR, of the best quality possible.
4) **Grating**　NUTMEG and CHEESE, especially PARMIGIANO (parmesan) should always be freshly grated and PEPPER should likewise always be freshly ground.
　　　　The difference between the packaged, already grated or ground and that done at the last minute is enormous
5) **Vegetables & Herbs** should always be fresh: the taste and texture of fresh ingredients are greatly responsible for the distinctive character of many Italian dishes.
6) **Made in Italy** Use only Italian Short Grain Rice for RISOTTO.

All of the illustrations were done exclusively for this book, executed with pen & ink, pencil, watercolor, colored pencil & pastel on handmade paper. Monuments, cityscapes, landscapes, food & domestic objects were drawn from life; copies of prints & other works of art were almost all rendered from the original but when this was not possible, a photograph was used.

Breadsticks

GRISSINI, eaten throughout Italy and in Italian restaurants all over the world are often, and rightly so, called GRISSINI TORINESI: during the 1800's Turin was sometimes called GRISSINOPOLI. According to popular legend, these crispy breadsticks were first made around 1670 by a baker there, Antonio Brunero, for the sickly young Duke of Savoy, Vittorio Amedeo II (1666-1732), when his doctor requested something easily digestible to stimulate his flagging appetite. One can assume that this new food had its desired effect for he was to reveal a strength of character and a sensitive intelligence that had remained hidden during his early years, especially after his father's death in 1675 when his French mother reigned with rather domineering tendencies. An active, resolute participant in European political and diplomatic events in the first quarter of the 1700's, he was crowned King of Sicily with great pomp in 1713, a title exchanged for that of Sardinia in 1720. He im-

plemented a variety of cultural and social reforms and promoted the separation of church and state: public, nonsectarian schools were opened and the Univesity of Turin, fonded in 1405 was expanded. In addition, some of this city's, and Italy's, most stunning baroque architecture was commissioned and it is amusing and pleasing to imagine that perhaps those simple GRISSINI made of just flour, water, yeast and salt had a role in these accomplishments. An alternate explanation attributes the GRISSINO'S origin to Vittorio's father, Carlo Emanuele II: in 1668, worried about the possible spread of an epidemic, he asked bakers to make a more hygienic bread and Brunero created these sticks which, as they contain less moisture than loaves and rolls, are less likely to get moldy and spoil. However, it seems that Brunero may not deserve all the credit given to him: in 1643, a Florentine abbot, Vincenzo Rucellai, wrote in his travel diary of a new "extravagant" bread, as long as an arm and very thin, that he saw and presumably tried in Chivasso, just outside of Turin. Thus, Brunero's invention was probably a variation of an already existing delicacy. According to Luigi Cibrario (1802-1870), statesman and historian from Turin, GRISSINI derived from thin, elongated breads weighing only about four ounces called GRISSIE made starting in the 1600's; in his "Storia di Torino", printed in Turin in 1845, he refers to these breadsticks with affection, expressing gratitude to the city's expert bakers who perfected the art of stretching dough into arm's-length, cord-like forms without it breaking. When the word GRISSINO began to be used is not known. The term most likely comes from the Piedmontese GHERSA, meaning both a line, row or sequence of similar things and a long, more or less cylindrical shaped bread, "the length of two palms of the hand", once common in the Region's rural areas. Long breads, in fact, are traditional in northern Europe while round ones are more typical of the south: GRISSINI, born at the northern tip of southern Europe, seem an extreme example of this difference. As Cibrario recognizd, much practice and manual skill were needed to make them and Turin's bakers were justifiably famous, as they are to this day. Like many other things, machines can imitate them but they cannot duplicate them.

Perhaps the biggest difference between the handmade GRISSINI of the past and today's is their flour. Flour is defined as the dry, dusty substance produced by grinding the fruit of cereals or legumes and although people have been eating fragmented grains in a variety of ways for thousands of years, fine powdery flour is a quite recent arrival in the history of food. Prehistoric societies crushed grains with a stone and archeological findings of teeth from that period, pitted and marked from friction with rough materials, show how coarse the kernels were and the bits of stone that got mixed in during the grinding made chewing even more difficult but, fortunately, things improved. Mortars and pestles were replaced by two rather massive, super-imposed stones, one fixed and one revolving, but it was not until the 19th century, when rotating metal cylinders began to be used, that the fine flour we now have was produced. Breaking the cereal's tiny grain is the only way of getting to its starchy interior, which accounts for from 60 to 80% of its total weight which, when crushed or ground, is reduced to a more or less homogeneous consistency that can combine with water to form a paste or dough. In spite of modern technological refinements and improve-

Detail from "A Discussion",(1892), oil painting by Giovanni Quadrone (1844-1898) from Mondovì (Cuneo). Exhibited at GAM museum, July 2002

*Two views of the **Ricetto**, early 1300's, Candelo, near Biella.*

RICETTI were born around 1300 as a defense against enemy invaders. Originally probably of wood, they became sturdy brick & stone structures consisting of towers, drawbridges & walls with moats & some took the form of a tiny village, as Candelo. They were particularly important in the plains, which lacked the natural defenses of hilly & mountainous areas.

A community's RICETTO served mostly as a safe storage for agricultual products, especially grain, & people paid a fee for putting food there but it was also a concrete expression of political autonomy, an initiative undertaken by residents for their security. Many RICETTI have disappeared, some incorporated into later constructions. Candelo's, beautifully restored, is a rare example of this type of fortification unique to the Piedmont, typical of the Canavese area.

ments the quality of stone-ground grain is often preferred for making certain traditional cookies, breads and polenta and interest in reviving this method has led to the restoration of a few of the Piedmont's old water mills.

In the past flour was not only coarser than today's, it was usually also darker. In the Piedmont, as elsewhere, only the wealthy could afford to eat white wheat flour and if ordinary people ate it, it was normally mixed with an inferior grain, usually rye, a combination so common it had its own name: BARBARIATO or BARBARIA. Rye was once extensively cultivated in this Region and for centuries was planted with wheat as a sort of ersatz crop rotation: since it needs fewer nutrients than wheat, the soil's vitality was less depleted, allowing more continuous cultivation. Well into the 1800's, at least 80% of the Piedmont's bread consisted of BARBARIATO; it disappeared with the introduction of modern fertilizing techniques and the traditional preference for white bread —wheat has always been the most desirable grain- facilitated its demise but GRISSINI were no doubt made from other than just wheat flour, out of necessity and not by choice. For those who could afford it, sifters were used to eliminate rougher bits of the grain: it is said that no one was permitted to use sifters finer than those of the bakers for the House of Savoy.

Although reputedly born to satisfy fundamental needs for survival, GRISSINI nonetheless enjoyed a certain fame and popularity and they continue to be relished. Two often cited examples of the Savoys' fondness for them are the purchase of a large container specially made to hold the breadsticks that Carlo Emanuele III took with him on his honeymoon in 1724 and Carlo Felice's (1775-1831) well-known habit of munching on them almost everywhere, even during theatrical performances. They

14

also attracted the attention of foreigners. In an anonymous book entitled "Viaggio Storico politico di Svizzera, d'Italia e di Germania" (c.1730) in addition to the author's account of the history and politics of Switzerland, Italy and Germany, "...little sticks of bread consisting entirely of crust..." are mentioned when the Piedmont is discussed. Napoleon discovered these "little batons" when the French invaded Turin in 1801 and liked them so much that he had them sent over the Alps after he returned to Paris for it seems his personal bakers were unable to reproduce them. For the French writer Antoine Claude Pasquin Valery, they were one of the first surprises awaiting the traveler in the Piedmont, very pleasing and digestible, providing one's teeth were good, and no more expensive than ordinary bread. This last fact was also noted by Friedrich Nietzsche who, while living in Turin for several months in the 1880's, wrote that the local population was exceedingly fond of them but he preferred bread rolls, with which he was more familiar.

In spite of the favor they received from the nobility, an emperor and notable visitors, GRISSINI are not mentioned in cookbooks until the 1850's, perhaps because bread, in general, is for the most part ignored. They are, however, specifically referred to in Giovanni Vialardi's cookbook, "Trattato di cucina pasticceria moderna credenza e relativa confetturia" printed in Turin in 1854 (subsequent editions were titled "Cucina borghese semplice ed economica") which has a recipe for ZUPPA PANATA, or breadcrumb soup: finely crushed GRISSINI are added to "good" hot broth, stirred until thickened, gently boiled for 15 minutes and served with a dab of butter, similar to ZUPPA BARBETTA (p. 93). Of much interest, considering it was published in 1864, in Trieste, outside the range of the Piedmont's influence, is Colombo Coen's "La Cuciniera universale ossia l'arte di spender poco e mangiar bene" (the universal cook or the art of spending little and eating well): it gives no recipe but describes GRISSINI as healthy and nutricious, of exquisite flavor and

1. Porta del Magazzeno Terreno   2. Porta del Magazzeno Superiore
3. Rampa per la salita de Carri al Piano Superiore

delicious with coffee, hot chocolate, broth and soups and, if made with butter, more delicate tasting but also more perishable. Dictionaries of that period are another source of information, an example being the definition in Francesco Cherubini's "Vocabolario Milanese-Italiano" (bilingual dictionary, Italian-Milanese dialect) published in Milan in 1840, which praises their great digestibility and warns against the spurious, inferior ones made in Lombardy.

These historical references confirm the GRISSINO'S prestigious position in the world of bread products. Yet another makes it seem almost sacred and comes from conversations that the writer Nuto Revelli had with rural Piedmontese women from 1979 to 1982, recorded in his book "L'Anello forte-La Donna: storie di vita contadina" (the strong link-women: stories of rural life) published in Turin in 1985. They describe the hardships, poverty and customs of country people, mostly before World War II, and one tradition, especially in the area of the PIANURA, or plains, was to bring a gift of GRISSINI to mothers just after giving birth, offering a very different, and touching, image of the atmosphere in which these breadsticks were eaten, and showing how precious they were for some people. Their digestibility was probably a factor, bringing to mind the young duke and the GRISSINO'S role in restoring health.

After the Second World War GRISSINI began to be eaten in the rest of Italy and now industrial production makes this once local specialty virtually a national food but Valery's word "surprise" still holds true: the Piedmont's are unique, different from those made elsewhere, which are usually thicker, more rolled than stretched, and offer breadstick lovers a memorable gastronomic experience. Neighborhood breadshops in cities and towns throughout the Region often sell freshly baked, fragrant, long slender examples loose, not packaged. They are normally "plain", classic flour, water and yeast although olive oil or suet may be added; without sesame seeds, onion, rosemary ect., their simplicity makes evident the baker's skill for their consistency and lightness need no extra ingredients. Even their paper bags are special, long enough so they need not be broken in two which of course does not effect their flavor, but eating them intact is somehow more fun. In restaurants and TRATTORIE PIEMONTESI one often finds handmade GRISSINI laid loose on the tablecloth in a neat cluster or attractively wrapped in a cloth napkin.

In Turin and its environs the GRISSINO is often found in company with a sort of variation of itself, the RUBATÀ. Its name comes from the Piedmontese term RUBAT, which was a type of primitive threshing machine consisting of a large wooden cylinder, fluted lengthwise, that by rolling over spikes of grain –it was normally pulled by horses- separated the kernels from their chaff. RUBATÀ means rolled and, in fact, these breadsticks are made by rolling the dough into pencil-like forms. They are shorter, denser and chewier than the more crumbly, crispy and flakey GRISSINI. At first the two seem quite similar but, with eating, their distinct qualities become very obvious. Some people have strong preferences for one or the other, some feel their differences determine how they are best eaten: dipped, dunked, crushed for soups or simply munched on their own.

Recipes for making GRISSINI at home occasionally appear in cookbooks though these are rarely Italian publications. I have never heard of anyone here making them, as one can bake homemade bread: the authentic GRISSINO cannot be produced without much practice and domestic ovens are inadequate for their extreme length. While many regional Italian alimentary products and ways of preparing them have been transplanted, with success, to other parts of the peninsula, the GRISSINO TORINESE is found only in the Piedmont due probably to the difficulty of acquiring the skill necessary for mastering this art and, perhaps, because few of these bakers have migrated elsewhere in Italy. Alongside the word PANIFICIO (where bread is made) the word GRISSINIFICIO sometimes appears on Piedmontese storefronts: these sticks are so good that even if Turin had not produced any other culinary treat, the city's fame would still be assured.

Grissini Vendor, *colored engraving by Gallo Gallina from "Costumi dei contorni di Torino" (traditions of the environs of Turin) published by Pietro Marietti in Turin, 1834. Gallina depicted laundresses, porters, servants, country people selling local wares, etc. Historic Archive of the City of Turin*

Piazza Santorre di Santarosa, Savigliano (Cuneo) This long, vaguely rectangular piazza was radically remodled in the 1470's when the facades of the buildings around it were transformed by constructing the porticoes we see today. These galleries, which moved the buildings' fronts forward to occupy more of the Piazza, made it possible to increase the living space of the floors above; in some cases, a single stretch of portico was so "maestoso" that an entire apartment could be housed above it.

Bagna Caoda

BAGNA CAODA, or hot sauce, is said to be the Piedmont's most characteristic dish which is a bit surprising since a typical meal in this Region includes several antipastos, both hot and cold, one or more pasta and main dishes plus cheese and dessert. BAGNA CAODA, instead, is a one-course repast, complete in itself but its classification as an antipasto confirms the predominent role that the Piedmontese give to their "appetizers" and verifies the belief that of the three culinary traditions that have influenced their cuisine, aristocratic, middle-class and peasant or country cooking, the third has been most important in creating today's CUCINA PIEMONTESE: BAGNA CAODA is decidedly rustic. This sauce, hot refers to temperature, not spicyness, is made by slowly cooking garlic, salted anchovies and olive oil and is eaten with a variety of vegetables, usually raw, dipped into the hot BAGNA. Though in the 15th century physicians began to cau-

tiously recommend eating fresh salad greens, the virtues of raw vegetables were recognized much later, making this dish quite avant-garde.

It is thought that BAGNA CAODA was created to celebrate the tapping of a year's newly made wine in early winter. Wine making has long been an important Piedmont industry and, as some of Italy's most prestigious wines are produced there, one could rightly expect a traditional dish to go with it. But, BAGNA CAODA is also associated with another event in the calendar of rural life, that is, the end of the farming season and the start of winter, the brief rest that lasted 'til spring thaws made it possible to once again till the soil. This time of year is particularly relevant for the vegetables eaten with BAGNA CAODA, as the onset of chilly temperatures and a touch of frost are felt necessary for them to reach their just maturity. In the past, the sauce was cooked in a wide terra-cotta pot with a handle, the DIANÈT or FOJÒT, nestled amidst a fireplace's smoldering embers, preferably oak, and how it was eaten was part of the festivity: everyone dipped the vegetables into the common pot, creating an intimate, shared experience, still characteristic of this dish. Nowadays BAGNA CAODA is no longer strictly associated with wine making. Thanks to mechanization, chafing dishes and fondue sets, it is eaten by many who have never picked a grape or even been on a farm. Although most common in grape growing areas, especially the Monferrato, it is made throughout the Piedmont and while locals admit that, given the quantity of garlic it contains, once is enough, they add that if they did not eat it even once, the year would seem incomplete.

A variety of raw vegetables (cabbage, Jerusalem artichokes, peppers, scallions...) and cooked ones (cauliflower, onions, potatoes...) along with bread are submerged into the steaming sauce but the true protagonist of this dish is the cardoon. In fact, this rather uncommon food is responsible for the earliest written references to a hot sauce with hints of BAGNA CAODA. The second of two recipes for CARDI in the 1775 edition of the anonymous "Il cuoco piemontese perfezionato a Parigi" (Turin, 1766) (Piedmontese cook perfected in Paris) ends with the note that they may be eaten with anchovies "melted" in hot oil. In the mid 1800's, Francesco Chapusot, head chef for the British ambassador to the Savoy court, offered eight recipes for this vegetable in his book "La vera cucina casalinga: sana economica e delicata" (Turin, 1851), a re-working of his "La cucina sana, economica ed elegante" printed in 1846 (why the "healthy, economical cuisine" changes from elegant to delicate and becomes "casalinga", or homecooking, is not clear); in one of these, raw cardoons are dipped into a hot sauce of oil, mashed anchovies and nutmeg and white truffles are added at the last minute. Subsequent similar recipes for this, as yet, nameless dish vary a bit –the spice may be eliminated- but none contain an essential ingredient of today's version: garlic is strikingly absent, perhaps because these books, as almost all historic cookbooks were for the middle and upper classes which deemed garlic a poor person's food.

Garlic belongs to the large Liliaceae family that, in addition, includes tulips, hyacinths and lillies. Garlic, whose name comes from the old English words GAR, meaning spear, for its pointed leaves and/or pungent odor and LEAC, or leek, is found on every continent. It does not grow in tropical environments but thrives in the Northern Hemisphere: centuries of adapting to different climatic conditions plus its ability to withstand the cold have let it move far beyond the limits of its original habitat, presumed to be Central Asia, from where it spread to Asia Minor, Egypt and, over time, across Europe. In the remote past it was imbued with supernatural powers: in his "Natural History", Pliny the Elder wrote that for the ancient Egyptians it was not only a food and condiment but, like the onion, was also sacred and invoked when making an oath and in Homer's "Odyssey", wild garlic, Allium moly, was the miraculous herb that Hermes gave Odysseus to turn his companions, whom the enchantress Circe had transformed into swine, back into humans. It is easy to dismiss such attributes as superstitious nonsence but garlic's effectiveness among primitive medicines - called the "peasant's pharmacy", it was eaten or made into lotions and potions and served as a cure-all for dandruff, epilepsy, toothache etc. and as an antiseptic and antidote- is supported by modern science: it is beneficial in treating hypertension, intestinal worms and parasites, bronchial and lung diseaes, nicotine poisoning and indigestion.

Evidence of garlic's importance for flavoring and healing are the medieval Piedmontese statutes and decrees obliging all farmers, landowners and sharecroppers alike, to grow it and fines for stealing it were higher than for most garden vegetables; in some places, the theft of just one head of it was punishable while in other, more lenient ones, taking three or more constituted a criminal act. The rich ate it only when its strong taste and odor were "ennobled" by the choice game and fresh vegetables it was cooked with; those unable to afford such luxuries ate more garlic, with little else. Thus, the original sauce for the wine tasting would very likely have contained it, but peasant cooking was of no interest to cookbook writers before the 20th century.

Many foreigners have an exaggerated idea of garlic's presence in Italian cuisine. It is actually used very sparingly, often removed after lending a bit of flavor during sauteeing or cooking and the region that uses it the most is the Piedmont. Most of Italy's crop grows in the south but, as garlic's taste and smell get stronger as it moves north, notable ones come from the Piedmont, Liguria and Emilia-Romagna. There are several types of wild garlic: some are planted for their beautiful flowers while others are troublesome weeds that, if inadvertently eaten by cows, give their milk, thus butter and cheese, a disagreeable taste.

Allium kerataviense
(garlic) Botanical Garden, Turin

The anchovy is one of the most important ingredients in the CUCINA PIEMONTESE. The word anchovy, like the Italian ACCIUGA, derives from the Greek term APHYE, meaning something small and indeed, this slender, silver-iridescent member of the Engraulidae family is around 14 centimeters long. Italians also call it ALICE, from the Latin ALLEC, meaning spoiled, putrified, decayed. For the ancient Romans, ALLEC was a tasty paste made from various types of decomposed fish and was basic for GARUM, their famous condiment which has been impossible to reproduce. For those who could not afford the spices added to make GARUM, ALLEC alone had to suffice. Used in many of their antipastos and to stimulate the appetite, ALLEC is thought to be the progeni-

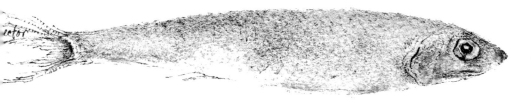

Engraulis encrasicholus
(anchovy)

tor of anchovy paste. Not only consumed fresh and spoiled, ACCIUGHE were also preserved in salt: they were a precious and convenient source of protein for Roman soldiers who spent long periods at sea and in his "Natural History", in the section "Remedies from Aquatic Animals". Pliny wrote that eating fish preserved in salt was useful for treating snake, insect and spider, especially scorpion, bites and for those of crocodiles, nothing was more effective. While their reputed therapeutic benefits eventually lost favor, salted anchovies continued to be prized for their high nutrition and became a profitable commodity.

Large schools of anchovies live in several European seas and the Atlantic, Pacific and Indian Oceans: the tastiest ones come from the warmest of these waters and those from the

Tyrrhenian Sea, along the coasts of Liguria and Spain, are the best. In the past, they ranked quite low in the hierarchy of seafood, long considered to be a poor person's food. Their diminuitive size may have influenced this negative attitude but, more importantly, since fish from lakes and rivers were easier and safer to catch than those from salty seas where the results of this activity were uncertain and unpredictable weather made it dangerous, fresh water varieties were more prized and usually reserved for the wealthy. Anchovies normally were salted as soon as they reached the shore after being caught. Alternating layers of whole fish and salt were arranged in wooden barrels that were covered with bricks or stones and left out in the sun at least two months while a sort of fermentation took place that conserved the contents for long periods of time. For Piemontese living in remote mountain valleys and hill towns, salted anchovies, and sometimes eels, were often the only aquatic form of food they knew; notations of tolls and taxes for preserved fish in medieval and renaissance registers show a constant pattern of supply and demand, a traffic intimately connected with salt.

Among the most heroic figures in northern Italy's culinary history are the Piedmont's ACCIUGAI AMBULANTI, salted anchovy peddlers, an activity born, like other seasonal itinerant trades, out of poverty and necessity for this Region's isolated alpine villages could not offer their inhabitants enough to eat all year long. For centuries, from September to March, women, children and old people stayed at home while male adolescents and men went to the lowlands, taking advantage of the winter pause in farming to work, among other things, as traveling salesmen and these anchovies were just one of the things they sold. Since at least the early 1800's this fish was the exclusive monopoly of people from a few tiny communities over 1000 meters in altitude located in the secluded cul-de-sac Valle Maira which extends some 60 kilometers east-west in the heart of the Cozie Alps, northwest of Cuneo, and this merchandise is associated with their descendents to this day.

While there is no exact explanation as to how this specialization came about, in his study of this valley's seasonal migrant workers, "Anciuìe e caviè 'd la Val Mairo", Diego Crestani suggests that they

Peis da Sal (Salt Scale), 19th cent. Museum of Arts & Trades of the Past, Cisterna d'Asti (Asti)

originally went to Liguria, to sell canvas produced around Biella to ship builders in Genova, Imperia and Savona and left these ports with salted anchovies which they easily sold on their way back home. Or perhaps it was hair peddlers: women in the Piedmont's mountain settlements normally sold their long tresses every year to such vendors who traded these braids and curls for the preserved fish while the hair went to London and Paris to be made into wigs, but, maybe this connection had to do with the very means of conserving the ACCIUGAI, that is, salt.

The salt used to conserve anchovies was as precious, if not more, as the fish. This crystalline substance is indispensible for humans and certain animals, such as bovines and ovines —the most severe monastic communities tried to do without it and failed- and its ability to preserve food and enhance its taste has made eating more pleasurable since the far distant past. Its extraordinary value can be seen by the fact that it was one of the first things that early medieval rulers regulated and taxed, often heavily, perhaps the oldest example being that imposed on both the vendor and buyer by the Lombard king, Liutprand, in 715; the Italian state maintained a monopoly on it 'til 1973. The Arabic word QABALA, a tax that was paid for a plot of land, is the origin of GABELLA, an Italian tax, usually on salt, that buyers and sellers paid and, similarly, the Hebrew QABBALAH, or cabala, refers to receiving , not something fiscal or material but, rather, instruction and tradition. Frequently, the head of every Piedmont family had to acquire a certain amount of salt for each person in his household, a duty reduced for fathers of more than 12 children and those doing military service. Such decrees served not only to fill the state's coffers, they also functioned as a population census, albeit imprecise. After the ancient Romans, no systematic demographic data was collected in Europe until the mid-1800's: in 1857, no longer associated with salt, the Piedmont carried out Europe's first "modern" census, relying on people's active collaboration and consisting of a sheet of printed questions quite like those asked today.

Monviso
(3841m)

After climbing Monviso on August 12, 1863, Quintino Sella decided to found the Italian Alpine Club

The Piedmont got most of its salt from the islands of Ibizia and Sardinia and from the Venetian lagoon, brought to the ports of Genova, Imperia and Nizza, or Nice (under the Savoy's domain from 1388 until ceded to France in 1806), where it was transferred to mules and carried across deep valleys and over high rugged mountain passes. The most direct, but steepest, route was over the Colle di Tenda (1870 mt.): probably first used by the Saracens around the year 1000, it remained fundamental for all sorts of goods for centuries. A crucial event in the history of the salt trade occurred in 1475 when, to facilitate its transport to and from southern France, the Marchis of Saluzzo, Ludovico II, had a tunnel dug through the 3841 meters high mountain Monviso, at the point of Colle delle Traversette (2882 mt.). Completed in 1480, the BUCO di VISO, or "hole of Monviso", is 75 meters long and two meters high and in spite of its dimensions and darkness, permitted traffic even during winter. As difficult as building this tunnel was, the value of salt made the cost and risks worth taking. Not surprisingly, smuggling was rampant and the onerous taxes encouraged contraband activity even though punishable with the death penalty. Anchovies, however, seem to have facilitated things for it is thought that the ACCIUGAI AMBULANTI from the Valle Maira provided the perfect cover for illegal salt: their fish were "packaged" in it and while all goods were subject to custom duties, anchovies were taxed less than salt and their quantities were less controlled.

Salted anchovies are essential for many Piedmontese dishes: they have more taste & character than those preserved in oil. They are sold in sealed tins, & keep for many weeks once opened if covered with their salt, as well as loose, by weight, from large barrel containers. They must be rinsed in water to remove salt, scales, head & tail & split open to remove innards & backbone. This preparation is more than compensated for by the remarkable way they evoke the sea, far more than those in oil.

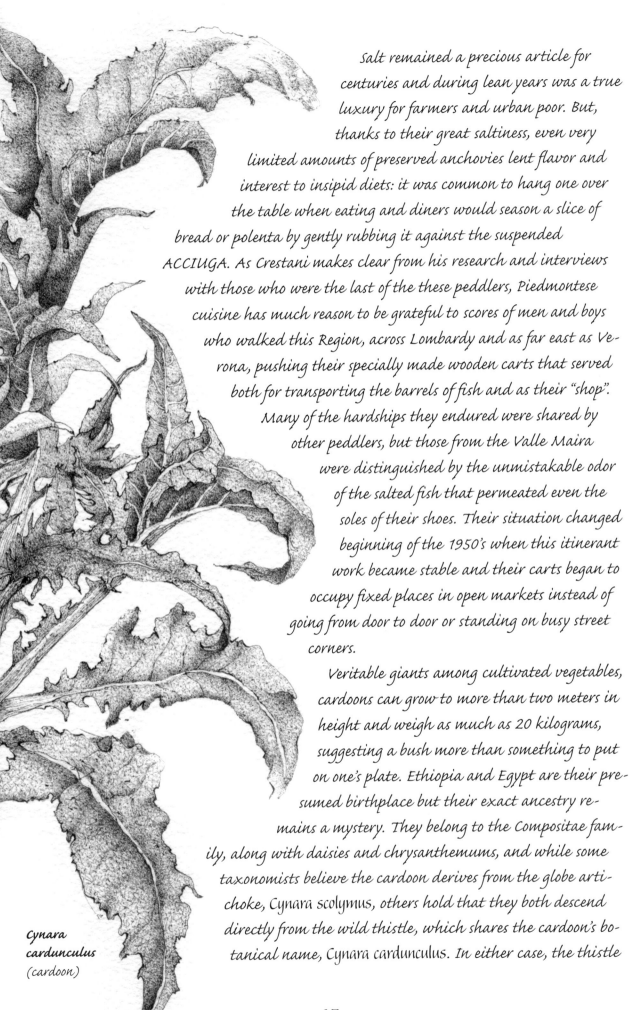

Salt remained a precious article for centuries and during lean years was a true luxury for farmers and urban poor. But, thanks to their great saltiness, even very limited amounts of preserved anchovies lent flavor and interest to insipid diets: it was common to hang one over the table when eating and diners would season a slice of bread or polenta by gently rubbing it against the suspended ACCIUGA. As Crestani makes clear from his research and interviews with those who were the last of the these peddlers, Piedmontese cuisine has much reason to be grateful to scores of men and boys who walked this Region, across Lombardy and as far east as Verona, pushing their specially made wooden carts that served both for transporting the barrels of fish and as their "shop". Many of the hardships they endured were shared by other peddlers, but those from the Valle Maira were distinguished by the unmistakable odor of the salted fish that permeated even the soles of their shoes. Their situation changed beginning of the 1950's when this itinerant work became stable and their carts began to occupy fixed places in open markets instead of going from door to door or standing on busy street corners.

Veritable giants among cultivated vegetables, cardoons can grow to more than two meters in height and weigh as much as 20 kilograms, suggesting a bush more than something to put on one's plate. Ethiopia and Egypt are their presumed birthplace but their exact ancestry remains a mystery. They belong to the Compositae family, along with daisies and chrysanthemums, and while some taxonomists believe the cardoon derives from the globe artichoke, Cynara scolymus, others hold that they both descend directly from the wild thistle, which shares the cardoon's botanical name, Cynara cardunculus. In either case, the thistle

Cynara
cardunculus
(cardoon)

27

Cardo Gobbo

generated these two very different varieties, interesting for their morphological and genetic qualities as well as their gastronomic ones. While the artichoke developed its upper, flower parts, the cardoon's modifications concentrated themselves below, in its leaves and stalk which multiplied and became ribbed, thick and fleshy. Fortunately, for those who prepare them, with domestication both plants lost almost all of the thistle's needle-like spines.

Like other plants, the cardoon spread from Africa throughout the Mediterranean world but has never been cultivated as much as the artichoke, perhaps because the cardunculus is very demanding. It is extremely sensitive to cold and needs fertile soil, rich in potassium and organic material; since it exploits all available nutritive elements, more than any other produce, in the past it could be raised in the same place only once every three or four years but modern fertilizers have changed this. Their seeds, which birds are particularly fond of, are sowed in April or May (in Sicily, as early as January) but before doing so, the earth must be plowed to depths of at least 40 centimeters as their robust roots develop deep, complex underground structures. Above ground, the plants require almost constant attention and the soil around them must be kept free of all extraneous growth, whether grass or weeds. By late summer their beautiful, fluttering wavy leaves and graceful tapering stalks are so heavy they lean over and farmers must intervene with one of three techniques that provide support and warmth and also bleach them. Two involve tying each plant with string or willow twigs, then wrapping dry straw or piling earth around the stalks, like a skirt, leaving only the upper leaves exposed; if necessary, they are protected from the rain. The plants remain vertical, shielded from the sun and their stalks become white, very tender and delicate tasting. Much of the Piedmont's crop, as in other parts of Italy, is grown this way but a third method serves for the "humpbacked" cardoon, or CARDO GOBBO, an extraordinary example of an already unusual vegetable.

Considering this plant's African origins and climatic needs, it seems rather strange that an area as un-Mediterranean as the Piedmont boasts two remarkable varieties of it. Those of Chieri are famous for their pleasing, slightly bitter taste while the Monferrato's SPADONE, or broadsword, is sweeter. For centuries, the banks of the Belbo River just north of Nizza Monferrato where this narrow

Cardoons *terra cotta decoration on house of Amadeo VI, 14th cent., in Rivoli (Turin). Similar tiles adorn many of the Piedmont's buildings. In a publication of 1910, the renowned local botanist, Oreste Mattirolo, called them MATTONI CARPOLOGICI, or "vegetal" bricks. For him, they were medieval artisans' glorification of nature's abundance.*

waterway widens a bit were covered with cane and reeds, used to make trellises for the grape vines on the surrounding hillsides but in the early 1900's local farmers began growing vegetables there and found the sandy soil very hospitable to cardoons. The nickname "humpbacked" comes from the way they are supported: by September, when they are too tall and heavy to stay upright, each plant is bound with string and gently leaned over into a slightly inclined furrow (so the water drains) dug next to it and the stalks are completely covered with the area's buff-colored soil for about 30 days leaving just the tips of their sinuous, silver-green leaves exposed. The CARDI "rebel" against their blanket of dirt and in their struggle for light, their stalks swell, becoming curved, "humped" and white. It is precisely its adaption to this difficult growing situation that makes this cardoon so tasty, tender yet crunchy: INGENTILITO, or refined, as the Italians say. Proof of its delicacy is the fact that all other types must be cooked, while the GOBBO is eaten raw; considered essential for the classic BAGNA CAODA. The art of cultivating the CARDO GOBBO is mastered over time and requires, for example, an understanding of how each year's soil has a different sand content which determines how deep the furrows will be and how much the plants are covered. Knowing exactly when to uncover them is also crucial for waiting one or two days can result in a crop of rotten cardoons. The CARDO GOBBO production is very limited and its yield very low: only 1/10th of the plant's weight is edible.

Not only dipped in BAGNA CAODA, cardons are eaten boiled, baked and fried, with bechamel or anchovy sauce or parmesan cheese, and have long been used for soup. A recipe for ZUPPA di GOBBI is included in Francesco Prato's book, "L'Arte di far cucina di buon gusto" (the art of tasty cooking) printed in Turin in 1793; he also recommends eating them with a green sauce or a fish one, which could mean anchovies. The four volume "La Nuova Cucina economica" (new economical cooking) by the Roman Vincenzo Agnolotti, (Milan, 1819) has a recipe that specifies the GOBBO or "cardo domestico" and he suggests using salted anchovies for sauces. His section on "useful warnings for cooks" advises never contradicting one's employer but instead, stating opinions with deference and respect and paying kitchen assistents promptly. He also strongly cautions against any financial involvement with artists but gives no hint as to why this group is singled out.

It has been pointed out that two of BAGNA CAUDA'S three essential ingredients -anchovies and olive oil- are not typical Piedmont products, although a few place names are testimony of the past presence of olive trees. A general warming of Europe's climate during the Middle Ages facilitated local authorities' interest in cultivating this tree: archival documents show that in some areas in the 1300's Piedmontese farmers were obliged to grow at least one and fines were imposed for damaging or cutting them. However, they were never very fruitful and most of this Region's oil came from Liguria and Provence, used only by the rich and, even then, sparingly and historians believe this was the case throughout Italy. Like other oils, it served mostly for making medicines, to give body to preparations composed of dried herbs, spices, eggs, ashes, ground seeds and minerals and animal parts and for lighting sacred lamps. Its scarcity and cost made alternatives desirable and though numerous nuts, seeds and plants were pressed for this purpose, walnuts were by far the best source and were once fairly common.

While the walnut's exact origins are difficult to trace, fossils dating from the late Tertiary period show that types quite similar to the ones we know today grew throughout Europe and then, like many other plants, disappeared from that continent during the last Ice Age but continued to fluorish in Western and Central Asia from where, perhaps aided by prehistoric people's migrations, spread north, east and west. Their cultivation probably began in the distant past in the Middle East and Asia Minor and then moved to Greece where they were called KARNON PERSIKON, or Persian nuts, in reference to their presumed place of origin. The ancient Greeks introduced them into Italy where the Romans called them Jovis glans, meaning Jupiter's acorn, and as their empire expanded, they took them to Spain, France and England. The word walnut may come from the Old English words WEALH, for foreign, and HNUTU, or nut, or from the Latin Gallia, or Gaul (from where it went to England) and nux, or nut. Geography continued to influence its name: today, common walnuts are called Persian, Circassian and English, the last due to the fact that they were unknown in North America before colonization and, as they first came in British ships, they were thought native to England. The walnut tree, NOCE in Italian, adapts to a range of climatic conditions and environments. It grows from the 56° parallel North to 10° South and, depending on exposure, as high as 1000 meters above sea level, but is a bit sensitive as to temperature: northern varities endure as much as 40° below zero and if the winter is not cold enough, budding is at risk,

Roman Amphora, 1st cent., reused for drainage system. Archeology Museum, Acqui Terme (Alessandria)

their production may decrease and morphology change but those in the Mediterranean suffer at 10° below zero and they must be sprayed during the summer against possible sunburn. During the Middle Ages walnut trees were very present throughout the Piedmont: they were planted in orchards and vineyards, amidst field crops, in meadows and courtyards and grew wild in forests. Their valuable fruit was protected by local laws and unauthorized gathering of nuts from the trees as well as those fallen to the ground was prohibited. An important source of nutrition for ordinary people –rich in protein, vitamins, lipids, fats and carbohydrates- they were also a profitable commodity sold locally and exported whole, shelled or as oil. This oil was not just for cooking, though in taste and quality is second to olive: in one of medieval and renaissance Europe's chief industries, woolmaking, it served to soften fibers and was also used to make soap and medicines and for dyeing and illumination. It was produced in a specially designed apparatus consisting of two grinding stones, a stove and a press that was sometimes installed as part of a water mill for flour. People would bring freshly shelled nuts to be crushed between the stones, their paste was boiled and pressed and the extracted oil collected in pails; to prevent fraud, laws stipulated how much oil a given amount of nuts should render. Medieval documents in some Piedmont archives include inventories of domestic possessions, one being a ROTA IN DOMO PER OLEO (domestic wheel for oil) suggesting that people also ground these nuts at home. Walnut wood, used for making furniture and tools, made the NOCE, in the words of a Piedmontese farmers' almanac of the 1840's, the most necessary of all trees for rural areas.

Thanks to modern transport and to southern Italians who migrated to the Piedmont after World War I, bringing their culinary culture with them, olive oil is now an integral part of this Region's cuisine. The great number of walnut trees mentioned in the English writer Thomas Coryat's

Glazed Ceramic Container used in the Piedmont for storing oil, 17th-19th cent. Museo Civico, Cuneo

description of his visit to Italy in 1608, is now much less: this fruit is still available, but no longer crushed for oil though older Piemontese can remember its distinctive pleasing taste and aroma. For a hint of this bygone flavor, a few chopped or crushed kernels may be added to the BAGNA CAODA as it cooks. Today butter is also added, tho at different moments. Some melt it immediately to cook the garlic, some do this in butter and oil, others in oil only, adding the butter at the last minute. Unanimity prevails, however, regarding how the garlic is cooked –very slowly, for 30 to 45 minutes, simmered rather than sauteed: it must not color and should become a creamy white paste. To mitigate its power, it can be thinly sliced and soaked in milk for about two hours before cooking which also makes it easier to digest. Bread is usually served along with the vegetables and is very useful for gathering the last drops of sauce; another way of finishing it is to scramble a few eggs right in the pot.

Bagna Caoda

~ 4 servings ~

Earthenware chafing pot
2 oz. BUTTER
6-12 cloves GARLIC minced, chopped or mashed
1 ⅓ cups OLIVE OIL
5 oz. SALTED ANCHOVIES rinsed, split open to clean & remove backbone

optional
3-4 WALNUTS, crushed or chopped
⅓ cup BARBERA wine, traditional in the Monferrato

1) Melt the BUTTER in the pot over low heat, add the GARLIC, & optional NUTS, & cook very slowly, stirring occasionally with a wooden spoon 'til it disintegrates: it must not darken. This takes about 40 minutes.

2) Stir in the OIL & ANCHOVIES & gently mash the FISH with the spoon. After about 10 minutes the mixture should have a uniform, creamy consistency. Add the optional WINE & serve.

VEGETABLES

RAW, cut into strips: cabbage leaves, sweet peppers, carrots, red radishes, Jerusalem artichokes; cardoons-once sliced, soak in cold water with a few drops of lemon juice to prevent darkening

COOKED, to be dipped with a fork: cauliflower, potatoes, onions, beets, turnips, roasted red peppers

BREAD & GRISSINI

Some people feel celery & fennel are too aromatic for this dish , but others include them.

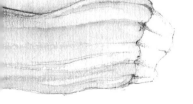

33

Antipasti

*W*ithin the extraordinarily rich world of Italian cuisine, that of the Piedmont is unique not only for many of its dishes, but also for the way and when they are eaten. Few other regions have its PIATTI UNICI, or one-course meals, such as BAGNA CAODA, FRITTO MISTO and BOLLITO MISTO, or the diversity of its cheese course, and none offers as varied and unusual an assortment of ANTIPASTI. Literally "before-the-meal", these appetizers, to an outsider like myself, are not just something to eat but seem to represent characteristic aspects of the Piedmontese natives that are expressed most tangibly through their cuisine. Although generalizing is always risky, the people of this Region are known as being serious, reserved, not given to ostentation, relatively indifferent toward appearances and packaging and the almost theatrical quality of social interaction sometimes found in other parts of Italy is less present here. But, when it comes to foods, their flavors, consistencies, contrasts, temperatures and presentation, the Piedmont offers a magnificent spectacle, to be looked at, smelled, savored, chewed and swallowed, and its ANTIPASTI are the perhaps the epitome of this.

In one of the most famous and esteemed contemporary cookbooks on this Region's cuisine, "La cucina del Piemonte", by the well-known gastronome Giovanni Goria, of a total of 369 recipes, 114 are for ANTIPASTI and they consist of a great variety of ingredients. One is struck by the absence in this, and other similar books, of a chapter on vegetables -CONTORNI, or side dishes- especially considering that Italy is famous for its flora, edible and not. However, they play a major role in ANTIPASTI: onions, peppers, cabbage, eggplant, zucchini and their flowers are stuffed and are themselves used to fill other foods and for making pies and FRITTATE, or omelettes. Stuffings, it is said, were born to use leftovers and "discards" and thus have economic along with alimentary importance but more interesting is the fact that recycling and recuperating these bits and pieces, giving them new life and dressing them up with garlic and herbs to turn them into appetizing morsels, requires creativity and ingenuity. This metamorphosis often entails elaborate, lengthy preparation and these ANTIPASTI are sometimes more complicated to make than other regions' main courses, and in larger por-

34

tions can be served for such. But, they are not all so intimidating: local salami and lard, sliced beets, INSALATA RUSSA, similar to potato salad, are often among these appetizers.

Many Piedmontese do not eat ANTIPASTI before their everyday dinner at home but a meal with invited guests almost always begins with them: traditionally speaking, the lack of this course would seem offensive to guest and host alike, which gives them a significant social function for they serve to show respect. Fortunately, for those who do not have the chance to eat in private homes, ANTIPASTI are easily available: many of them can be bought ready to eat in GASTRONOMIE, or gourmet shops and delicatessens, and restaurants of various levels serve them a la carte and with fixed-price menus, which, more common in this Region than elsewhere in Italy, are not designed for tourists. Eaten this way one quickly discovers their formal aspect, usually absent in private homes where various ones are offered together, as waiters bring them separately, in a carefully determined order, so that two different ones are not eaten simultaneously. Since it often seems as if a certain measure of ceremony is an almost unconscious pleasure, this imposed progression adds a touch of ritual to the sensual and gastronomic enjoyment of these dishes. Proof that they are among the Piedmont's most interesting foods is seen in the fact that restaurants occasionally replace a normal meal with a wide selection of ANTIPASTI and many bars offer an increasingly growing array of them, sometimes making dinner unnecessary. They are also part of another uniquely Piedmontese custom, the MERENDE SINOIRE, an unusual example of how this Region makes simple eating something special: of humble origin, this informal late afternoon-early evening snack once consisted of little more than salami, salted anchovies and SOMA D'AJ –crusty bread rubbed with garlic and sprinkled with olive oil and salt- but nowadays these are joined by a variety of ANTIPASTI, cheese and, of course, wine and supper is forgotten.

The number and the diversity of the ANTIPASTI, the fact that some are eaten hot, some cold, with the fingers or with silverware, makes them even more fun and tempting. Perhaps it is this almost playful aspect that, in the Piedmont, where things are taken rather seriously, seems to make them as if the alter ego of the natives, a means of expressing their joie de vivre lightheartedness in a very concrete way.

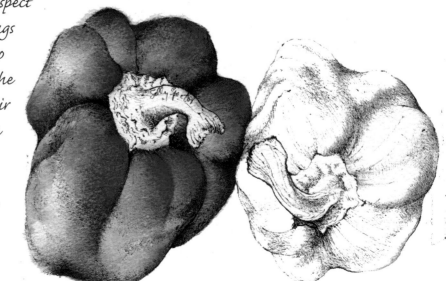

The following pages present a few of the Piedmont's most classic ANTIPASTI.

Stuffed Cabbage Leaves   Pess-Coj

~ 4 servings ~
if served as a Main Course, double the proportions

8-10 large, outer Savoy CABBAGE leaves,
4 oz. cooked BEEF (roasted, boiled or braised),
finely chopped
3 oz. SALAMI or MORTADELLA, finely chopped
2 TB. fresh minced PARSLEY
a few leaves fresh BASIL & ROSEMARY
2-3 TB. grated PARMESAN CHEESE
1 EGG, beaten
OLIVE OIL or BUTTER

1) Drop the CABBAGE leaves in abundant boiling salted water & boil 'til soft & wilted. Drain & lay on a towel to dry. Two of them may be chopped & added to the filling.
2) Combine the MEAT with the HERBS in a bowl, add the EGG & CHEESE & the optional chopped CABBAGE & mix well. If necessary, add a dash of SALT & PEPPER.
3) Form the filling into 8 little cylinders & wrap a leaf around each one or put the filling directly on the leaves and roll them into a fish-like, oval shape. Tuck the ends in well so the filling does not fall out.
4) Arrange the filled leaves in a baking dish & dribble a bit of oil on them. Bake for 30 minutes at 325°. Turn them over & bake 'til lightly browned. Or, fry them in heated BUTTER, turning 'til golden. Serve hot.

In the Canavese area BOILED RICE is sometimes added to the filling.

The stuffed leaves vaguely recall a fish, thus the name PESS-COJ, Piedmontese for "fish-cabbage".

Coat of Arms of the Cavassa family from the CASA CAVASSA, Saluzzo. A fish swimming upstream is a repeated visual motif in this elegant Renaissance home's decoration. Built in the 1400's, renovated in the 1500's, restored in 1885, it was given to the city & is now a museum.

36

Stuffed Zucchini Flowers

Caponet

~ 4 servings ~
12-16 ZUCCHINI FLOWERS
stuffing for CABBAGE LEAVES
BUTTER for cooking the stuffed
FLOWERS

    1) If necessary, clean the FLOWERS very gently with a soft damp cloth. They are extremely fragile & rinsing can damage & wilt them. Carefully remove their inner stem.

    2) With a spoon, fill each FLOWER with some stuffing. Close them by bringing their tips together & giving them a slight twist.

    3) Melt the BUTTER in a large frying pan over moderate heat. When the foam subsides, add the FLOWERS, turning them to brown all over. Drain a moment on absorbent paper & serve hot.

Minced Raw Beef   Carne Cruda

~ 4 servings ~
The excellence of this dish is due not only to the quality of the meat but also to its texture & consistency. It should be mincd by hand, not by machine. Cutting it by hand gives it "character", "personality", that is completely lacking in the perfect homogeneity & uniformity of that produced by grinders & blenders &, in addition,this method makes it more tender & helps retain its moisture. Not surprisingly, however, it is painstaking & takes much longer than machines.

14 oz. very lean VEAL (top round or shoulder), 3-4 TB. OLIVE OIL,
{**optional ingredients: ** 1/3 -1/2 of a GARLIC clove, minced
1 SALTED ANCHOVY, rinsed, boned & minced, pinch of CINNAMON or NUTMEG,
3-4TB.LEMON JUICE: added 10 minutes before serving, the MEAT'S red color will turn a bit gray}

    1) With a very sharp, long-bladed knife cut the MEAT into little cubes, then mince these 'til they are about the size of grains of rice. Pounding is also recommended.

    2) Put the OIL & a dash of SALT & PEPPER in a bowl & gently beat together with a fork. Mix in an optional ingredient.

    3) Add the MEAT & mix with the OIL 'til well combined. Serve at room temperature.

Tuna Pâté

Pâté di Tonno

~ 4 servings ~
7 oz. canned TUNA
2 SALTED ANCHOVIES, rinsed & boned
2 oz. BUTTER, slightly softened
2 TB. fresh minced PARSLEY, LEMON SLICES

1) Mash the TUNA & ANCHOVIES a bit with a fork &
press them through a strainer with the BUTTER. A blender can be
used but take care not to produce a sauce: the mixture should have a
smooth but firm consistency.

2) Form into a sausage shape, wrap in aluminum foil & refrigerate 7-8 hours.

3) Serve sliced, garnished with PARSLEY & LEMON slices.

Anchovies With Green Sauce

Acciughe Al Verde

~ 4 servings ~
15-20 SALTED ANCHOVIES *
3-4 GARLIC cloves, minced
3-4 TB. minced fresh PARSLEY
1 hard-boiled EGG YOLK, minced
2-3 TB. OLIVE OIL, 1-2 TB. WINE VINEGAR

1) Carefully rinse the ANCHOVIES to remove
salt & scales & split them open to remove back
bone, keeping the tiny fish whole. Drain on paper
towels.

2) Mix the minced ingredients together in a
bowl. Stir in the OIL & VINEGAR to make a dense sauce.

3) Arrange alternating layers of FISH & SAUCE, finishing with a topping of SAUCE.
Serve on toasted bread or crackers: some people let the prepared dish sit a few hours at room temperature
before serving.

*For those not accustomed to SALTED ANCHOVIES this dish can taste rather strong, thus, fewer
fish can be used

Veal with Tuna Sauce

Vitello Tonnato

~ 4 servings ~

VITELLO TONNATO, veal with tuna sauce, is a popular summer dish in a few parts of Italy & one of the Piedmont's most famous & preferred ANTIPASTI, eaten there all year long. In this Region, the veal may first be marinated in a mixture of wine, vinegar & herbs or may be simmered immediately in the marinade ingredients, as is usually done in other places. Particularly well-suited for buffet & stand-up meals, it can be prepared in advance: the tuna sauce keeps the cold meat very moist & tender.

1 LB. boneless piece of lean VEAL, top round or shoulder

MARINADE
2 BAY LAUREL leaves
a few fresh SAGE leaves
3 CLOVES
1 ONION, coarsely chopped
½ cup WHITE WINE VINEGAR
DRY WHITE WINE & WATER in equal amounts to cover MEAT

SAUCE
3 hard-boiled
EGG YOLKS
6 SALTED ANCHO-
VIES, rinsed & boned
7 oz. canned TUNA
CAPERS: 2-3 TB.
minced & a few left
whole for garnish
1 TB. WHITE WINE VINEGAR
juice of one LEMON
about 1 cup OLIVE OIL

1) Put the VEAL in a ceramic or glass container (not metal). Add the HERBS, ONION & LIQUIDS & let marinate, covered, in a cool place, but not refrigerator, for 24 hours. Turn the MEAT over two or three times.

2) Put the VEAL in a heavy pot. Strain the marinade liquid & pour it over the MEAT, adding WATER to cover if necessary. Add a pince of SALT, bring to a boil, lower the heat & simmer, covered, about 1 ½ hours. Remove from heat & let the VEAL cool in its broth.

3) With a fork, mash the YOLKS, ANCHOVIES & TUNA together & push them through a sieve or finely mince with a half-moon cutter: a blender can also be used. Put them in a bowl & add the CAPERS, LEMON JUICE & OIL. Mix well & dilute with a bit of broth: the sauce should be smooth, creamy & not too thick.

4) When the MEAT is cool, cut it in thin slices. Place a veil of sauce on a serving platter, arrange a layer of sliced MEAT over it, cover with some sauce & continue arranging alternating layers, finishing with a topping of sauce. Garnish with the whole CAPERS, cover with plastic wrap & refrigerate at least 1 hour. This dish can be prepared several hours, even a day, in advance & kept in the refrigerator: in this case, remove from the fridge 1 hour before serving.

Capers growing in the Botanical Garden of the University of Turin. Present throughout the Mediterranean area & in tropical Africa & Asia, capers grow wild in many parts of Italy. In the Piedmont they often flower from old stone walls with sunny exposure.

Stuffed Onions "Canavese"   Cipolle Ripiene "Canavese"

Stuffed onions are most closely associated with Ivrea, long famous for its CIPOLLINE, but this is a popular dish throughout the Piedmont. As with stuffings in general, some liberty may be taken —ingredients range from beef, sausage & pork liver to pumpkin & rice- & some people add a sprinkle of powdered bitter chocolate & cinnamon but this version is so unusual it is best not to vary it too much. The filling for STUFFED CABBAGE (p. 36) may also be used.

~ 4 servings ~

2 ½ LB. medium ONIONS
6 oz. AMARETTI cookies, chopped
MILK
1 white BREAD ROLL, cut into small pieces
2 TB. OLIVE OIL
4 oz. BUTTER
grated NUTMEG
1 EGG
3 oz. SUGAR
3 oz. grated PARMESAN CHEESE
2 ½ oz. RAISINS
possibily, grated BREAD CRUMBS

TOPPING
1 EGG
½ TB. SUGAR
1 TB. grated PARMESAN CHEESE
¼ -½ cup MILK, used for soaking the AMARETTI
    buttered baking pan

1) Peel the ONIONS, remove their thick outer layers & cut them in half. Boil them in abundant salted boiling water for 15 minutes. Drain & set aside to cool.

2) Soak the AMARETTI in MILK to cover & the BREAD in tepid water for 10-15 minutes. Drain the cookies & reserve the MILK, squeeze excess moisture from the BREAD & set aside.

3) Make little cups out of the ONIONS by scooping out their centers, leaving about ¼ inch width of skin around them. Take the most tender, inner parts, finely chop them & sauté with the OIL, a bit of BUTTER & a pinch of NUTMEG, SALT & PEPPER. Let cool.

4) In a bowl, beat together the EGG & SUGAR. Melt the remaining BUTTER & add it to the bowl along with the drained AMARETTI & BREAD, the RAISINS, CHEESE & sauteed ONIONS & mix well. If the texture seems too dry, add a bit of the AMARETTI MILK, if too moist, add a bit of BREAD CRUMBS.

5) TOPPING: Beat the EGG & SUGAR together in a bowl, add the CHEESE & stir in the MILK. Preheat oven to 250°.

6) Fill the ONIONS with the stuffing, making sure the top is slightly rounded, not flat. Arrange them in the baking dish. Drop a spoonful of topping on each ONION & bake 1 ½ hours. During the final half hour open the oven door occasionally for a few seconds to let out excess moisture. When done, let sit 10 minutes, then serve.

When domestic ovens were a rarity, people prepared these onions at home & brought them to their local baker: after he finished baking his bread the onions were cooked in the heat remaining in the oven.

scale, late 1800's: Blacksmith Museum "OFICINA BERGO", Chiaverano (Ivrea). This museum is housed in an old iron "factory" where, since the early 1700's blacksmiths & mechanics produced scales, weights & other precision instruments for a variety of professions: carpenters' tools & fixtures, agricultural implements, equipment for miners & masons, kitchen utensils, knives, keys, gates, nails, railings, in short, any iron & copper object that was necessary for executing a myriad of activities. A water wheel provided the energy for turning lathes, drills, grinding stones & other machines which, tho now not in operation, could still function. In the past, there were numerous such workshops in this area, famous for their excellence in metalwork.

The double numbers on this scale indicate weight in both the metric system & that used in the Piedmont before this new system was introduced in the mid-1800's, but which took some time to be understood & accepted: thus, it could be read by everyone.
In the 1790's, the French government assigned four experts the task of creating the metric system of weights & measures, based on a miniscule fraction of the earth's circumference. Three were French, the other was a mathematician from Turin: Luigi Lagrange (1736-1813), of international fame, contributed to many aspects of this subject – teaching, analytical works, number theory, differential calculus etc. & was a founding member of what became Turin's Royal Academy of Sciences.

Stuffed Onions   # Cipolle Ripiene

~ 4 servings ~
4 large ONIONS
½ LB. minced BEEF or VEAL
BUTTER
3 TB. grated PARMESAN cheese
1 EGG
GRAPPA
Buttered baking pan
Preheat oven to 400°

1) Peel the ONIONS, remove their thick outer layers & boil them in abundant salted WATER for 15 minutes. Drain & let cool.

2) Lightly brown the MEAT in a bit of BUTTER.

3) Remove some of the pulp from the center of the ONIONS & finely chop it. Mix the pulp with the MEAT, add the CHEESE, a pinch of SALT & PEPPER & the whole EGG. Combine the ingredients to a homogenous consistency.

4) Fill each ONION half with the mixture & top with a dot of BUTTER. Arrange them in the pan & sprinkle a few drops of GRAPPA on them. Pour 3-4 TB. of hot WATER or BROTH in the pan & bake 40-50 minutes.

To give the ONIONS a golden crust, brush their tops with a beaten EGG & sprinkle with BREAD CRUMBS or finely crushed GRISSINI. These ONIONS are usually eaten hot but are also delicious tepid or cold.

Island of San Giulio,
Lake Orta

Literally, IN CARPIONE means pickled, which does not necessarily evoke much gastronomic interest but the Piedmont offers a quite grand version of this preparation: fish, vegetables, veal, turkey, eggs... are lightly fried, then marinated in vinegar with onions and herbs that flavor and preserve them.

The name derives from CARPIONE, a sendentary member of the Salmonidae family whose preferred habitat is muddy lake bottoms: in Italy nowadays it lives almost exclusively in Lake Garda. To exalt its tender flesh and eliminate hints of earthy sediment, it is usually prepared pickled, or CARPIONATO, and other fish found in the Piedmont are similarly well-suited to this method, such as the carp and whitefish of Lake Orta, river trout and, especially, the TINCA, or tench, a European

42

member of the Ciprinidae, or carp, family. The 270 meters high plain of Poirino, a town between Asti and Turin, is home to a particularly distinguished one, the TINCA GOBBA DORATA, or humpbacked golden tench. Thanks to geological events, numerous tiny lakes and ponds formed there: for centuries, their stagnant waters served mostly to irrigate fields and quench the thirst of the oxen that plowed them but they were also perfect quarters for this TINCA which loves to bury itself in the hughly nutricious sediment it heartily devors, eschewing muddy naterial, that carpets these small basins. Because of its very low oxygen requirements, the TINCA survives in environments where no other fish could and it can live for years in what for other creatures is putrid water. Poirino's farmers often raised tench in the nearest pond for private consumption, like barnyard chickens, but after the abandonment of rural for city life in the 1900's, this fish was much forgotten. However, its tasty, delicate meat has been rediscovered and the TINCA DORATA IN CARPIONE is now a specialty in local restaurants.

"Pickled..."

"In Carpione..."

MARINADE

1 TB. OLIVE OIL
1 large ONION, thinly sliced
2-3 GARLIC cloves, left whole
10 fresh SAGE leaves
about 2/3 cup each WHITE WINE VINEGAR & WATER*
optional
2 BAY LAUREL leaves
6 JUNIPER BERRIES, slightly crushed

Cover the FISH, MEAT or ZUCCHINI with the marinade. Let sit from 6 to 24 hours.

TURKEY, CHICKEN, VEAL

3 slices TURKEY, CHICKEN or VEAL, about 3 1/2 oz. each
1-2 EGGS, beaten
2-3 TB. BREAD CRUMBS
2 TB. OIL
2 TB. BUTTER

Dip the slices in the EGG, sprinkle with SALT, then dip them into the BREAD CRUMBS. Heat the OIL & BUTTER & fry the MEAT on both sides. Arrange the slices in one or more layers in a glass or ceramic container.

FISH

2 freshwater FISH, about 12 oz. each
OIL for frying FISH

Clean the FISH: head & tail may be removed, tho this is never done in Italy. Heat OIL very hot & cook FISH 5-6 minutes on both sides. When done, sprinkle with a bit of SALT & arrange in one or more layers in a glass or ceramic container.

ZUCCHINI

1 LB. small ZUCCHINI
OIL for frying
MARINADE recipe

Cut the ZUCCHINI lengthwise, very thinly. Heat the OIL very hot & fry the ZUCCHINI, a few pieces at a time. As soon as they are done, transfer to a glass or ceramic container.

ZUCCHINI WITH EGGS

The ZUCCHINI IN CARPIONE are delicious on their own but are often accompanied by FRIED EGGS, one for each person. The EGGS are fried in BUTTER, laid over the fried ZUCCHINI & they are marinated together.

*It is essential that the best quality VINEGAR be used for CARPIONE: it is as important as the quality of the FISH, MEAT & VEGETABLES.

Vinegar, from "Tacuinum Saitatis"(book of health), late 14th cent. manuscript based on the work of 11th cent. Arab physician Ibn Botlan, from Baghdad. This Latin version, known as "Il libro di Casa Cerruti" (book of the Cerruti family), now in Vienna's National Library, contains illustrations by a northern Italian artist, probably Piedmontese or Lombard. The text describes therapeutic properties of plants (herbs, vegetables, fruits, grains), animals (fish, game, fowl), & cheese & sometimes, their negative effects, concepts that were the basis of health care 'til the birth of scientific medicine. According to this "Tacuinum", vinegar reduced excessive bile, soothed painful gums & stimulated the appetite; when boiled, its vapors liberated plugged ears; distilled, it killed worms & warmed, held in the mouth, relieved toothache. As for cooking advice, it recommends marinating fish in vinegar for 6 days: for the elderly, it should first be steamed but for passionate young men, boiling is better.

Grilled Peppers With Anchovies
Peperoni alle Acciughe

~ 4 servings ~
2 PEPPERS, red or yellow
SALT
2-3 GARLIC cloves, minced
4-6 TB. OLIVE OIL
4-6 SALTED ANCHOVIES,
rinsed & boned

1) Grill the PEPPERS: they will be very sweet, tender & easy to digest. This can be done with a barbecue or on top of the stove by placing a slightly raised grill over a burner. The PEPPERS should be close to the flame —you will soon hear little popping sounds— & turned so their skin blackens & blisters all over: it will be difficult to do this uniformly as the heat reaches flat sides more easily than curved indentations. They will give off liquid & get very soft & wilted. This proces should take about 20 minutes. When blackened, immediately wrap them in newspaper which helps them retain moisture & facilitates peeling them. After 10 minutes, remove the paper. Slip or pull off their skin with fingers & cut them in half. Remove stem, seeds & white pulp & rinse in cold water to eliminate any remaining burnt skin. Slice into strips 1 inch wide, sprinkle with SALT & drain in a colander at least one hour.

2) Put the GARLIC & OIL in a pan & cook over low heat 3-5 minutes: the GARLIC must not brown. Add the ANCHOVIES & mash them with a wooden spoon; stir about two minutes or 'til they melt into the oil.

3) Arrange the PEPPER strips on a serving plate & spoon the sauce over them. They may be served immediately or left to sit a few hours.

Outdoor Market, Piazza San Francesco, Acqui Terme (Alessandria) In the distance is the octogonal bell tower of the Basilica of St. Peter: presumably of early Christian origin, the church was renovated in the 11ᵗʰ cent.

Born in Peru, **peppers** were introduced into Europe in the 1700's. In the early 1900's they began to be cultivated on a large scale in the Piedmont, particularly in the fertile flood plain south of Turin where extraordinarily tasty & beautiful examples now grow. The most renown are the QUADRATO (square), CORNO (horn), TROTTOLA (whirligig) & TUMATICOT (sort of a squashed sphere). Their diverse forms make them well-suited for various preparations & they are very present in this Region's cuisine

45

The hamlet of **Lucedio**, near Trino, in the province of Vercelli, is the site of a once illustrious Cistercian abbey founded in 1123 by Raniero Marchis of Monferrato who had monks brought over from the Abbey of La Ferté in France, born 10 years earlier, to be its first inhabitants. Thanks to donations & privileges received from Popes, Emperors & Monferrato's noble families, the **Monastery of Santa Maria di Lucedio** became one of the area's wealthiest, with extensive terrain that the monks transformed into a flourishing agricultural enterprise. Its possessions along the banks of the Po River were particularly significant for it is said to be where, in the late 1400's, rice was first cultivated in the Piedmont.

Not only expert farmers, the monks also
exploited the River's waters for irrigation &
built numerous canals for this purpose:
during its most florid period of activity,
64% of the Monastery's farmland was rice
fields. In 1784 the Abbey was closed & its
property ceded to the Order of Saints
Maurizio & Lazzaro & eight years later,
the Dukes of Savoy were named
beneficiaries. Its present owners have
maintained the Abbey's original character
& tho' its terrain is much less than its once
87,000 acres several varieties of rice are
grown there. Of the Romanesque monastery,
only the octogonal tower remains; the
church was rebuilt in the 1700's.

Rice   Riso

The flood plain of the Po River, known as the PIANURA PADANA or the VAL PADANA, the plain or valley PADANA —from Padus, the river's name in Latin- begins in the Piedmont and extends through Lombardy, Emilia-Romagna and the Veneto. The Po, protagonist of this fertile plain and Italy's most important river, starts near the French border at the foot of Monviso, the majestic, isolated pyramid-shaped mountain (3841 mt.) that dominates the Piedmont's PIANURA and from there flows eastward for 672 kilometers until it empties into the Adriatic Sea just south of Chioggia. In the remote past the Greeks called this river Eridano, whose meaning remains a mystery, and the ancient tribe of Liguri, who were the first to inhabit this area, called it Bodinus, meaning exceptionally deep and long, as they imagined this great river to be: it was eventually named Pado, the Gallic word for the pine trees that once covered Monviso. Thanks to its waters, much of the VAL PADANA is home to some of Italy's most flourishing agriculture, an activity that dates back at least 4,000 years as shown by ancient stone carvings, plows and sickles.

The Etruscans, famous, among other things, for their agricultural achievements, were the first to regulate the PIANURA'S numerous waterways, almost all tributaries of the Po, and their efforts to drain and irrigate this territory were continued by the Romans who also introduced the use of manure to fertilize the soil. But things changed in the 5th century when the Roman Empire fell and tribes from northern and central Europe crossed over the Alps and invaded Italy. The hydraulic works that had made the Po Valley so fruitful were abandoned; the intruders were more

The Plowman, bronze Etruscan statue, 5th cent. b.C. Museum of Etruscan Art, Villa Giulia, Roma

adept at hunting than tilling the soil and fields that had been sowed for hundreds of years for lack of maintenance laid waste and while chaos reigned, were overtaken by bushes, brambles and swamps. Things improved slightly with the subsequent development of feudalism which brought some social order but, nonetheless, many people fled urban settlements to seek refuge in hill towns, remote mountain areas and in the lagoon that would give birth to Venice; those who stayed often died in local warfare or from diseases and epidemics. Nature was left free to run its course until, around the year one thousand, a fortuitous combination of events led to a general reawakening and one of the many aspects of life in the VAL PADANA that was to benefit was agriculture: the key to its rebirth was water...draining, distributing and regulating water.

Traina per condur il Terreno mosso, coi Buoi

...rm Machine, pulled by oxen & guided by a person, ...d for smoothing uneven ground: woodcut from ...nti giornate dell'agricoltura et de'piaceri della ...a" (20 days of agriculture & the pleasures of ...ntry life) by Agostino Gallo, 16th cent. nobleman ...n Brescia. First printed in 1550 with the title ...n Days", it was "13 Days" in 1556 & in 1559 ...re was an appendix of seven more. The ...nitive edition of 1572, "20 Days", was dedicated to ... Serene & Magnanimous Prince Emanuele ...berto of Savoy for, among his other virtues, an interest in ...roving agriculture: his promotion of land reclamation & ...gation resulted in more efficient & productive farming in the Piedmont. ...m edition of 1573, Venice. Marciana Library, Venice

In Italy, land reclamation is called LA BONIFICA, from the Latin bonus, or good, correct and facere, to do or make, and refers to centuries of efforts to increase and protect farming by eliminating unhealthy marshes, reinforcing river banks and getting water from where there is too much of it to where there is not enough. Religious instituions played a leading role in the early history of the BONIFICA in the VAL PADANA and Benedictine and Cistersian monasteries in the early 1100's were among the first to drain sodden ground. They frequently received extensive tracts of land donated by wealthy feudal families that were, however, usually barren, uninhabited and unfit for planting which the monks, aided by local peasants, redeemed for grazing and plowing, often creating properous and profitable agrarian communities. Municipal authorities knew that hungry, underfed citizens were more likely to rebel than those whose stomachs were full which motivated them to follow the monks' example and thus medieval civic administrators undertook costly —both financially and physically- public works: constructing ditches, dikes, moats and large and small canals with locks improved farming conditions and they also served strategic, social and economic purposes. They were a defense against the constant threat of invaders for the sudden opening of locks to flood fields could halt foreign troops as in 1859, when this action blocked the Austrians near Vercelli; in times of peace they turned water mills and if wide enough were navigable and thus stimulated commerce.

The Piedmont built several irrigation canals during the 13th and 14th centuries and the first navigable one was opened in 1468: the 72 kilometer long Naviglio d'Ivrea branches out from the Dora Baltea River into numerous waterways that irrigate the Vercelli plain before reaching the Sesia River and facilitated traffic between these two important cities. Unfortunately, wars, foreign occupation, famine, pestilence and the high cost of upkeep hindered its full use until the 1600's when the ruling Savoys restored it. These pioneering monuments of hydraulic engineering let people and goods move more quickly and cheaply than ever before and reach new external markets, opening the way to increased trade: gastronomic culture also grew as products previously unavailable began, for those who could afford them, to influence local cuisines. The crucial relationship between urban and rural societies was forming, in which the latter provides food for the former that, in turn, governs the countryside and regulates the exchange and sale of its agricultural products. In the Piedmont, strangely enough, one of these eventually would be rice.

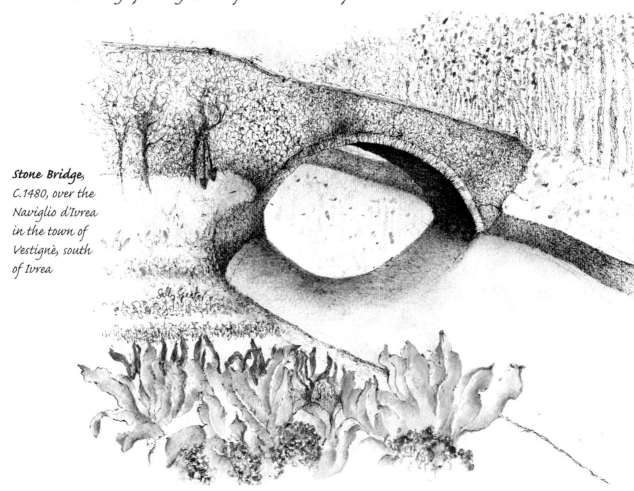

Stone Bridge, C.1480, over the Naviglio d'Ivrea in the town of Vestignè, south of Ivrea

The word rice, like the Italian RISO, derives from the Greek ORYZA which comes from VRIHIH, the Sanscrit term for this grain. It was likely first brought to the Western World in the 3rd century by Alexander the Great's soldiers who discovered it, as they did sugar, when they reached India, presumed to be its birthplace, and took it to Greece when they returned home. They, and the Romans, imported Indian rice via Syria and Egypt, although for them it was not a food but, instead, a costly, precious commodity appreciated for its symbolic and therapeutic qualities. Since remote times it has represented fertility and abundance —Italians toss it at weddings- and giving someone a little bag of rice was once a sign of respect. Considered a remedy for digestive problems, for centuries it was eaten almost exlusively by the firm and sick people. Documents show that in the 9th century it was re-exported from Sicily elsewhere in Europe which probably explains why it was often thought to be a Sicilian food.

Rice was first planted in Europe in the 10th century, in Spain, introduced there by the Arabs. When the Aragonese took over Sicily and southern Italy in the 1400's rice was cultivated in both areas, as well as in Tuscany, but without satisfying results. Things proved quite different in the Po Valley lowlands however, where some of the most prized varieties of rice were created and prosper today. By 1480 it was growing in Lombardy and soon spread into Emilia-Romagna, the Veneto and the Piedmont: merchants around Vercelli and Novara were already exporting this new grain by 1525 for it turned out that these areas' apparently unfavorable environment offered unexpected benefits. This is the world's most northern rice crop; normally it grows in tropical weather conditions, hot, humid and very rainy where irrigation is often unnecesary, between 40° North and South of the Equator, but here it thrives at 45° North. Adapting to this chillier climate requires a longer, slower growing cycle which, along with the Piedmont's loose, rich soil helps make Italian rice more nutricious and flavorful than other types. Most of the success that this crop enjoyed, however, was

Irrigation Canal – wooden locks:
Posana, near Canale Cavour (Novara)

due to the intelligent
distribution of water, of
which rice needs vast amounts,
though a minimum of excess can be
harmful.

A unique hidden feature of the lower Val Padana is the presence of countless underground springs, formed when slowly flowing subterranean water tables meet impermeable terrain and their horizontal movement being blocked, spurt upwards. In the Piedmont these
RISORGIVE or FONTANILI, "resurgences" or "little fountains", are more numerous just south-
west of Turin but those around Vercelli and Novara are the most prolific: in 1860 it was calculated that near Novara more than half of the 70,414 acres of irrigated land received water
from FONTANILI while the rest came from canals fed by rivers and torrents. Both the temperature of this water, from 10-12°C., and its flow remain constant: it never freezes and provides
the thermal protection that rice must have to sprout and grow there.

Exploiting the FONTANILI, draining swamps, constructing dikes and embankments,
digging canals and ditches and equipping them with a system of locks and gates were costly
undertakings, requiring the collaboration and expertise of engineers, surveyors and masons
and once realized, these complex interventions must be constantly monitored and maintained. The ingenuity of these works, which succeeded in making unproductive land fertile, were greatly admired by the famous English agronomist, Arthur Young, when he visited the Piedmont and Lombardy in the late 1780's but they were only worth doing on a
large scale and for a uniform crop such as rice, beyond the means of small independent
farmers with tiny plots of land and an ox for plowing. The expansion of rice had been much

hindered by the belief that, since it flourished in swamps where nothing else could grow, it caused epidemics and disease. Thus, planting it near populated areas was often prohibited, though the ill health associated with it was due as much to workers' poor diets and unhygienic living conditions as to the rice paddies. Although cultivation spread slowly, the Piedmont's rice was sufficiently famous to attract the interest of Thomas Jefferson who, when in Italy in 1787, succeeded in smuggling some of it back to the United States in order to try planting it there: nowhere, however, has its quality ever been matched. In the 1800's Novara and Vercelli were produc-

Locks, Canale Cavour, named for Count Camillo Benso Cavour (1810-1861) A leading participant in Italy's political events & instrumental in its unification, Cavour was also extremely involved in agrarian activity & a founding member of the ASSOCIAZIONE AGRARIA which favored more freedom of exchange & more open markets for farm products. Of the many projects he promoted, such as nursery schools, increased railroad connections & the construction of the first great tunnel through the Alps, the Fréjus (1857-1871; 12,849 mt. long), one of the most important was for a canal, proposed in 1854 but events such as the Crimean War & Cavour's untimely death halted this undertaking: begun in 1864, it was inaugurated in 1866. The Canale Cavour branches from the Po at Chivasso, irrigating the plains of Novara & Vercelli 'til it reaches the Ticino River in the Lomellino. Its regulated water supply keeps this land justly moist making it possible to maintain a perfectly balanced degree of fertilization: 50% more rice was produced, 30% more corn.

ing such significant quantities that, thanks greatly to serious private investment administered by manager accountants, Italy's first example of "capitalist" farming was underway.

From October to March the fields around Novara and Vercelli could easily be mistaken for normal farmland but a closer look distinguishes subtle variations in ground level...tracts of land, called CAMERE, or rooms, separated by straight, narrow ditches and embankments that exploit the terrain's natural, virtually imperceptible decline as it gently extends to the Adriatic Sea. The product of precise measuring, these slight gradations are integral to the clockwork-like mechanism that irrigates and drains the paddies, based on an intricate, sophisticated system of locks and movable barriers that control and regulate the waters which, from April to September, transform this landscape from dry clumps of light brown soil into perfectly still, rectangular "lakes" framed by low grassy dikes.

While farming in general seems magical considering that from tiny nondescript seeds comes a cornucopia of flavors, shapes, textures and colors that nourishes humans and animals alike, rice growing is particularly fantastic for this plant lives first like a fish, under water, and then emerges, like a flower, its long, tapering emerald-green leaves gracefully curving over the slender shadows they cast on the surface. Planted in April, by July, when seen from a distance these leaves are so dense that the water surrounding them is no longer perceived, their wet environment revealed only by the croaking of frogs and aquatic birds such as solitary gray herons, equally elegant whether still or in flight. By late summer the paddies are a thick carpet of mature golden spikes that seem to extend to the horizon. But, while rice's growing cycle and setting may excite the imagination, its cultivation was once back-breaking; for centuries, every phase of it –pre-paring and leveling the land, sowing, weeding, harvesting, threshing, husking- was done manually, with the occasional aid of oxen and horses and in-termittent attempts to mechanize some as-pect, such as a rice thresher invented by a lo-cal engineer, Rocco Colla, in the 1830's, but which did not have great success. Motorized ma-chines finally took over after World War II: to bet-ter maneuver them, the single rows of trees around the CAMERE as seen in paintings and old photographs were cut, and it is said they also blocked the sun.

Although rice needed fewer animals and permanent farmhands than other cereal crops it required a great number of temporary laborers, especially for cleaning and weeding the paddies, which revolutionized agriculture in the lower Pianura Padana: paid migrant workers, albeit poorly paid, began to replace the centuries old institution of MEZZADRIA, or share-cropping, that characterized traditional dry farming. In the early 1900's women be-gan to join the men and boys in the RISAIE, or rice fields, many of whom left to work in the factories just opening or were recruited to fight wars, and they quickly took over the most fa-tiguing chore –removing the weeds and algae that, starting in June, flourished in this damp environment and would steal the plants' nourishment, and even suffocate them, if not eliminated. Called MONDINE, from the verb MONDARE, to clean and remove the skin or rind of something, they worked every day for about six weeks, barefoot, knee-deep in muddy water in the company of frogs, snakes and mosquitoes, bent over the precious plants, an activity immortalized in works of art in which the pleasing patterns their wide-brimmed hats create lend the scene a deceiving beauty. The fifty-person teams of MONDINE, who came mostly from Emilia-Romagna and the Veneto, spent long hours in

Rice Fields in Winter, Balocco, in the irrigated plain north of Vercelli & west of Novara near Canale Cavour

55

extremely difficult conditions. Nonetheless, the RISAIE offered a chance to earn some money, go to a new place, meet new people –women's lives were very limited- and sometimes fall in love and stay there and despite the hard work, the camaraderie of this collective life made it a happy experience and many MONDINE willingly returned year after year. In addition to their contribution to Italy's agriculture, they played a leading role in this nation's labor history for in Vercelli, in 1906, they won the right to an eight hour workday, the first of such victories in Europe. Now they are but history: motorized machinery, genetic research to create varieties more resistent to disease and parasites, fertilizers and insecticides mean that today, two or three people can do what, fifty years ago, required forty workers.

Official recognition of rice's importance came in the 1900's when the STAZIONE SPERIMENTALE di RISICOLTURA was inaugurated in Vercelli and since then, scientists and other experts working there have succeeded in improving various aspects of this grain, creating tastier, healthier, more productive plants. Many people consider Italian rice superior to all others: the most famous varieties, recommended for RISOTTO rather than soups or sweets are CARNAROLI, ARBORIO and VIALONE NANO. In 1931 the ENTE NAZIONALE RISI was founded with the aims of promoting and publishing this food both in Italy and abroad and of encouraging economic and technical development related to its cultivation. After a new center for studying rice was opened in Mortara, situated about midway between Vercelli and Pavia, in neighboring Lombardy, the original one became a branch of the ISTITUTO NAZIONALE di CEREALICOLTURA (national grain institute). Recent work has revealed that rice is not only nutricious, low in fat etc.: its cultivation helps reduce the production of methane gas which is in part responsible for the dangerous warming trend that now threatens our planet. Thus, eating it is even more beneficial than previously thought.

Rice did not become an everyday food in Italy until the 1900's. While it is called for in a few recipes in the anonymous book "Il cuoco Piemontese perfezionato a Parigi" (the Piedmontese cook perfected in Paris) first printed in Turin in1766 –simply cooked in veal or vegetable broth for making MINESTRE, or soups, or enriched with egg yolks or seasoned with sugar and salt to be served as a side dish, or used for a sweet pudding-pie- some 20 years later it was still most appreciated for its ability to "sweeten and condense acidic bile and counteract diarrhea" as recommended by the Florentine Ignazio Ronconi

Emblem of the National Rice Board

56

in his four-volume "Dizionario d'Agricoltura" published in Venice in 1783. And, even when rice began to be freed of its associations with sick people, its consumption was hindered by the taxes and protective tariffs imposed by the numerous autonomous governments throughout Italy in defense of local products. Although a basic food since the remote past for at least 60% of the world's population, many of whom had, and have, little else to eat, prior to the 20th century the only poor people who ate rice in Italy were those who worked in the paddies and they usually had only the discards: immature, broken, defective grains in limited quantities, used mostly to make watery MINESTRE flavored with whatever vegetables were available. But, thanks to improved standards of living, these rudimentary soups gave birth to the Piedmont's most distinctive rice dish, a hearty, tasty combination of rice and beans called PANISSA in Vercelli and PANISCIA in Novara and similar versions, with different names, are eaten in nearby Lomellina, now in Lombardy but, in the 1700's, part of the Piedmont. Its name derives from the word PANICO, meaning foxtail millet and millet, and once referred to food made from any flour, from ground chestnuts to dried legumes to grains, cooked in boiling water, broth or milk, an example being the Ligurian polenta-like dish called PANISSA, made from ground chickpeas and still eaten today, now often called FARINATA, from FARINA, or flour.

In the Piedmont's rice growing areas, the local RISO is often sold in canvas or cotton bags.

Panissa

~ recipes on page 66 ~

Paniscia

*N*o longer watery soups, PANISSA and PANISCIA are thick, more a bean RISOTTO than a MINISTRA: that is, a small amount of rice is not added to boiling liquid and cooked 'til done. Rather, rice is toasted with sautéed onion, lard or local salami (butter and olive oil are optional), red wine is added and perhaps a bit of pork rind and then boiled in broth added gradually, stirring often, until this liquid is almost completely absorbed. The main difference between PANISSA and PANISCIA is their broth: the first uses beef broth or the water the beans were boiled in, the second uses broth made from slowly cooking the beans with a variety of vegetables, all added to the rice. While in the past the Vercellese used SALUGGIA beans, named for the nearby town where they were cultivated, and the Novarese used BORTOLOTTI, today the latter are standard for both versions. The small SALUGGIA variety is rarely grown now: its tendency to disintegrate during cooking and its lower yield led to its being replaced by the excellent BORTOLOTTO, both being similar to cranberry beans, legumes of the genus Phaseolus vulgaris.

Legumes are among nature's most generous creations. The largest of the three sub-families of Leguminosae is the Papilionaceae, whose hundreds of genuses and thousands of species include beans, peas and lentils. Since the remote past their pods and seeds have been an important source of nourishment for people, animals and even the earth itself since, while these plants feed on nutrients provided by the soil they

Phaseolus vulgaris

grow in, thanks to a bacteria that lives on their roots, they give off nitrogen through a process called nitrogen-fixing. Thus, they replenish and enrich the ground for subsequent crops and were crucial in the development of rotating them, one of agriculture's greatest discoveries, and they are also used for green manure. Their high protein content explains the nickname "poor man's meat" and many people who could not afford animal protein depended on legumes for this essential substance, and still do today.

The word legume comes from the Latin legumen, meaning anything that can be gathered and, in fact, these plants are a very reliable crop: sowed in the spring, they do not risk the damage that late, extreme winter weather can cause and their versatility is remarkable. When very young, the whole tender pod and its seeds can be eaten; when more mature, they are separated, the external part, leaves and stems used for forage while the internal fruit can be boiled or roasted and finally, when fully matured, beans can be stored, dry, for several months making the Papilionaceae a valuable food when fresh vegetables are scarce. They were often ground into flour to make porridge —another name for legumes is pulse, from the Latin puls, meaning a thick soup- or combined with grains to make bread. And, as the 14th century Bolognese Pietro de'Crescenzi wrote in his "Ruralium commodorum libri" (on farming), they had a cosmetic use as well: to clean and beautify the skin, he wrote, some people washed themselves with this flour. Their commercial value is seen in the fact that in the Piedmont during the Middle Ages beans, and sometimes lentils, were protected, strictly controlled products. It was often illegal to export them or sell them to FORESTIERI —anyone from a different, even nearby, town- and there were heavy fines for stealing them, with more severe punishment if stolen at night. Sometimes legumes served as money, given to hired workers as salary.

During the Middle Ages and Renaissance, differences between the rich and poor were not only material: they were also thought to be distinguished by physiological differences, especially regarding vital organic processes. Fava beans cooked in milk and served with meat were eaten by the wealthy but other types were judged too coarse for the supposdly more delicate, refined stomachs of the privileged, fit only for the grosser digestive systems of common people. Well into the 20th century some traditional "peasant" dishes, such as bean and pasta soup, continued to be shunned by the middle and upper classes, a prejudice now overcome.

Farm Implements, woodcuts from "Ruralium commodorum libri" by Pietro de' Crescenzi. A jurist by profession, he left that work in 1299 to devote himself to rural life. His book, considered the most important agrarian work of the Middle Ages, is based on ancient writings (Caton, Varrone, Columella) & his own experience. The Latin original was soon translated into Italian & then into French, English, German etc. Marciana Library, Venice.

Detail from **Stained Glass Window** depicting St. Anthony Abbot & the donor, Antonietto Barutelli, attributed to 15th cent. master glassmaker Antoine de Lonhy from Grugliasco, near Turin. Made for the Church of St.Peter in nearby Pianezza, this panel, with another of St. Peter, is now in the Museum of Palazzo Madama, Turin. In the past, pigs were smaller & darker than today's, with longer legs, smaller ears and more boar-like snouts

In addition to rice and beans, the other essential ingredient of PANISCIA-PANISSA is pork. I was not raised in a kosher home but it was sufficiently Jewish for me to have had more contact with chicken fat (Italian Jews used mostly goose fat) than with lard or suet. The only form of pork that ever entered our house was the bacon my mother very rarely bought, much to the delight of my sisters and I. I cannot recall ever seeing my parents eat it and I did not think about pig's meat as having more life than as crispy fried strips eaten with one's fingers or as the "B" in a bacon, lettuce and tomato sandwich. Pork chops, ribs or roast were never considered alternatives to beef, chicken or lamb. Once I expanded my alimentary horizons and began to eat and prepare "foreign" dishes, I found that personal preference keeps me from being a true lover of the enormous family of hams, sausages and salami but living in Europe has made me appreciate the importance of these pork products and research in culinary history makes clear that this much maligned animal, denigrated for its suppposed lascivious and unclean habits has given humanity not only sustenance, but much flavor as well. In Italy, where almost every zone has its own particular INSACCATO, salted pork "in a sack", a bit of rind, lard, suet, ham or sausage is fundamental for a variety of soups, sauces and stews; in the Piedmont, as elsewhere, less fresh pork is eaten than preserved and sausage and lard are often part of cold antipastos. Vercelli and Novara's contribution to this category is SALAME D'LA DUJA: salami conserved in suet to keep it soft and stored in a terra cotta vase called DUJA in Piedmontese dialect, glazed both inside and out. Like other traditional INSACCATI it can be difficult to find today and fresh sausage is used instead.

Fat is a requisite for much cooking and many people distinguish northern Italian cuisine from southern by the use of animal as opposed to vegetable fat but this difference is less profound than it seems. Although much of central and southern Italy produces olive oil, for centuries it was a priority of the well-off, used for seasoning and for frying, while lard and suet were the national cooking greases, here, as elsewhere in Europe. And, even after Italian cooks gradually began using butter in the 1500's, pork maintained the dominant role it had had since antiquity: raising pigs was relatively easy as they eat almost anything and their generally docile nature adapts to a wide range of environments, from the open space of forests and meadows to the confines of muddy courtyards and thus, in the past, even urban dwellers fattened a pig for private consumption.

The ancient Romans were very fond of pork, extolled by Pliny the Elder in his "Natural History" for, depending on where pigs lived and what they ate —acorns, chestnuts, barley, legumes etc.- their meat offered "fifty different flavors" whereas other animals had "just one". Other edible quadrupeds, such as sheep, cows and goats provided wool, milk and cheese and pulled carts and plows, but the raison d'etre of pigs was their flesh and fat. The only ancient cookbook we know of, called "De re coquinaria" (about cooking), compiled in Rome around the first century A.D., said to be by Apicius, a person associated with lavish banquets, includes several recipes for preparing pork: suckling and adult pigs were eaten stuffed, boiled, roasted, baked and as sausage. A favorite Roman delicacy survives only etymologically and gave us the word porcelain, PORCELLANA in Italian, from the Latin porca, or female pig: they boiled its vulva which became not only tender, but also white and transluscent, like the precious ceramic ware later named after it. Apicius' work was not discovered 'til the mid-1400's and had little, if any, effect on European cuisine at that time.

Although the gastronomic aspects of swine are clearly their most important features, these animals also had spiritual significance in the ancient world and were portrayed on

Detail from "**PEASANTS WITH OFFERINGS**", frescoe by Giacomo Jaquerio (1375-1453) from Turin, in the Church of St. Anthony of Ranverso, just west of Turin. The hermit monk Anthony (c.251-356) spent most of his life praying & meditating in the Egyptain desert & is famous for overcoming violent spiritual & carnal temptations. His emblem, a hog, is said to be a symbol of sensuality overpowered & also refers to his followers' dedication to caring for the sick. It seems that in the late 1100's, the relics of St. Anthony miraculously cured a case of herpes zoster, the terrible virus caused by eating grain, especially rye, infected with the poisonous fungus called ergot, common in the Middle Ages. A hospital was built in his honor & monks of his order devoted themselves to treating this malady by covering the blisters with pork rind; they had special rights to raise pigs for this purpose. The hospital of Ranverso, founded in the 1100's is one of Italy's oldest.

votive bas-reliefs and sacrificed during agrarian rituals. In fact, the Italian word for pig, MAIALE, is thought to derive from the name of the eldest and most beautiful of the seven celestial nymphs known as the Pleiades, the goddess Maia, mother of Hermes, in whose honor pigs were sacrificed. Vestiges of this ritual were passed on to the ceremonial butchering of hogs that, 'til recently, was an important event in the calendar of rural life which took place in November and December, at the close of the farming season. Most of their meat and fat was salted, preserved to eat during the cold winter ahead –the word larder, now the place for general provisions, originally referred to where lard was stored- while those parts not suited to conservation, such as blood and internal organs, were the basis for a festive meal consumed immediately. Pigs, however, were not limited to country life.

As a result of a warming of Europe's climate from about 750 to 1215, its population increased, which led, especially in northern and central Italy, to the development of urban communities, made up mostly of merchants and artisans who, 'tho many had a little vegetable garden, neither farmed nor hunted. They did not produce their own food but, rather, depended on rural people for it and this metropolitan minority profoundly affected the vast majority of Italians who, 'til the 20th century, were involved in some aspect of agriculture. Alimentation became commercialized: crops were raised, not just to fulfill the contracts of sharecroppers and tenant farmers and to nourish one's family, but to be sold or exchanged at markets and fairs. Key figures in this new food chain were PORCARI, or swineherds.

As early as the 7th century PORCARI tended the pigs of rich feudal lords, roaming the oak-filled forests that, even if private property, could be used upon payment of a tax, usually a quantity of gathered acorns or one-tenth of the grazing pigs which sometimes wandered onto tilled fields, but any damage

Quercus pedemontana

Piedmont Oak, lithograph from 'Herbarium Pedemontanum juxta methodum naturalem disposition" (plants of the Piedmont) published in 1837 in Turin by Luigi Colla. One of the Piedmont's leading 19th cent. botanists, he was a member of scientific societies in Italy, France, England, Bohemia & USA.. Library of Regional Museum of Natural History, Turin

they did was compensated for by the manure they left. Their numbers were so great that medieval woods were normally measured not in length and width but in how many hogs they could sustain. The PORCARI were highly valued for their knowledge and understanding of forested areas, as seen in the heavy fines for wounding or killing them. During the later Middle Ages they also worked for city dwellers who hired them to raise a pig or two to slaughter for the winter but their profession was on the way to extinction, victim of revolutionary changes in agriculture.

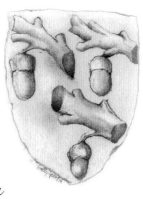

Coat of Arms on the holy water basin in the 14th cent. Cathedral, Asti, made from a romanesque capital of the earlier, 11th cent. church

Thanks to improvements in farming techniques in the 13th and 14th centuries —more rational fertilization and crop rotation, better implements- wheat began to replace grains such as millet, foxtail millet, spelt, sorghum and rye that were easier to cultivate but far less nutricious, a change judged one of the most important events in agricultural history. Forests in the Po River's plain were cleared and pastures transformed into wheatfields which meant eviction for grazing animals. The little livestock there was moved to the hills and mountains where forage was usually richer than in the lowlands and the animals were safer, less vulnerable to thieves, but the life of pigs became decidedly less arcadian. Some moved to farmyard pens, but most migrated to cities where they wandered loose, making the PORCARI unnecessary: documents from the 11 to the 1500's show that controlling them was a constant challenge for municipal authorities. Not only did their excrement pose hygienic problems, their undisciplined movement created traffic jams and norms were repeatedly passed in the Piedmont, as elsewhere, in an attempt to remedy this chaotic and dangerous situation.

In spite of the problems they caused, pigs were of great value, for pork was the only type of meat many Italians knew: beef was only eaten when bovines were too old for plowing and milking, mutton, when their fleece no longer made good wool and fresh meat, mostly game, was usually reserved for the rich and privileged. In 14th century Turin, for example, if a pig was killed and the

"Peasant Herding Pigs & Sheep", detail from a "Digestum vetus" treating legal matters such as commercial exchange, sale of animals etc. Now in Turin's National Library, this illuminated manuscript was produced in Bologna c. 1340: medieval archival papers show many transactions between Bologna & the Piedmont from 1270-1345 including a "Digestum" sent to Chieri via Genova by two merchants from the first city with a warehouse in the second. It is intriguing that it was executed when members of the noble family d'Acaja, from Pinerolo, were living in Bologna.

63

person responsible not found, its owner was compensated with public funds, a policy that became very costly due to the great numbers of these itinerent animals. Laws requiring swine to have custodians and iron rings in their snouts in order to herd them were often ignored and fines for any damage they caused did little to discourage their presence until finally in 1543 the city approved an ordinance confiscating all vagabond swine. An exception was made, however, for those branded with a red T, for TAU, indicating they belonged to the order of the Brothers of St. Anthony, which, because of its role in caring for the sick, had permission to raise pigs for therapeutic use: pork fat was a remedy for various ills, especially ergotism. While their animals could move freely, all others were confined to pens or closed courtyards, thus ending what had been a picturesque but bothersome aspect of daily life. Hogs were now slaughtered at butchers' stalls scattered throughout cities and towns, where their meat and other edible parts were sold. Very little was thrown away —even their eyes and ears were eaten- but there was still some refuse to eliminate, which the constant threat of plagues made lethal. Thus, this activity was moved to a fixed site on the periphery of communitis. Butchers, who had formed guilds as early as the 1200's in some parts of the Piedmont, were regulated by laws to ensure the freshness and quality of the meat they sold —it had to be inspected, protected from flies but visible to customers- and

Piazza Maggiore, Mondovì Piazza
The old part of this city, called Mondovì Piazza lies at an altitude of 550 mt., situated 150 mt. above the new part, known as Mondovì Breo. The long, irregular **Main Square** is framed by porticoed buildings, mostly from the 14 & 1500's. Private dwellings, cafes, shops & food stores such as the Gastronomia-Salumeria (delicatessen, salami, sausage) help this Piazza maintain its sense of vitality.

against fraud, common tricks being
pumping air into hams to swell them
and passing off inferior cuts as choice
pieces. Amazingly enough, little changed 'til the late
1800's, when modern concepts of hygiene and sanitation were
introduced and refrigeration made it possible to keep meat fresh.

An interesting testimony of pork's importance is the book printed in Turin in 1820,
written by Francesco Toggia (1752-1825), a Piedmontese veterinarian who was responsible
for this Region's military animals: "Intorno all'educazione, miglioramento e conservazione
delle razze de' porci" (the education, betterment & conservation of hogs) was the first
monograph to treat the raising and well-being of pigs. An example of modern, enlightened
veterinary science, Toggia's work includes concern for his subjects' emotional state; he encouraged farmers to consider their sensitive, sociable, loyal nature and, indeed, in the following decades, a growing recognition of how treatment of animals influences the quality of
their meat –and milk- was expressed in other agrarian publications.

Panissa ~ Vercelli

PANISSA & PANISCIA may be described as very thick soups or very moist RISOTTI & when talking about them with the locals, one senses their affection for these dishes, often made at home but little known outside the rice growing area. In the past, when there was less quantity & variety of food, PANISSA-PANISCIA had almost a symbolic significance, eating them in company was a sign of friendship & well-being. Restaurants & TRATTORIE around Vercelli often have PANISSA on

Paniscia ~ Novara

the menu but PANISCIA must usually be ordered a day ahead. The traditional salami used for them, SALAME D'LA DUJA, is named for the ceramic pitcher it was conserved in: in Piedmontese dialect DUJA is such a container, normally for wine. The SALAME was put in the DUJA & covered with melted suet, an ancient storage method that kept the pork meat so soft, it seemed almost fresh: difficult to find today, fresh pork susage is an acceptable substitute.

Fresh BEANS, BORLOTTI or CRANBERRY, are best, but dried ones, soaked overnight , may be used instead

~ 4 servings ~

PANISSA

2 oz. PORK RIND

12 oz. fresh BEANS, podded

1 QT. BEEF BROTH

2 cups WATER

2 TB. OLIVE OIL

1 TB. BUTTER

2 ½ oz. LARD, minced

2 ½ oz. SALAME D' DUJA, minced

1 large ONION, sliced

12 oz. ITALIAN RICE, for RISOTTO

optional 1 glass RED WINE

1) Blanch the RIND in boiling water, scrape it & put it in a pot with the BEANS, BROTH & WATER. Cook, covered, over low heat 'til the BEANS are soft & their skin begins to split.

2) Sauté the OIL, BUTTER, LARD, SALAME & ONION 'til the ONION is wilted.

3) Stir in the RICE & when toasted, add the optional WINE, stirring 'til absorbed. Add a ladle of BROTH & BEANS, stir 'til the mixture becomes "dry", add another ladleful & stir. Continue adding BROTH & BEANS as the liquid is absorbed 'til the RICE is cooked, stirring almost constantly. It should be done in about 20 minutes. Add all of the remaining BEANS, a pinch of PEPPER, & serve.

A wooden spoon with a point is recommended when making RISOTTO for it succeeds in gathering the rice grains from around the bottom of the pot better than a perfectly rounded one. Official instructions say to stir the rice constantly while cooking to keep it from sticking but some people like the taste & consistency of "pot-stickers" & thus let up a bit on the stirring.

PANISCIA

2 oz. PORK RIND

coarsely chopped:
1 stalk CELERY
1 medium CARROT
½ head SAVOY CABBAGE
3 ripe TOMATOES
   optional 1-2 LEEKS

8 oz. fresh BEANS, podded
1 ½ QT. WATER
2 oz. BUTTER

finely chopped:
2 oz. BUTTER
small ONION
3 ½ oz. SALAME D'LA DUJA

10 ½ oz. ITALIAN RICE, for RISOTTO
1 glass RED WINE, preferably Barolo

1) Blanch the RIND in boiling water, scrape it & cut into thin strips.

2) Put the RIND, VEGETABLES, BEANS, WATER & a pinch of SALT in a pot. Cook over moderate heat 2-2 ½ hours.

3) In another pot, melt the BUTTER & sauté the LARD, ONION & SALAME in it. Add the RICE & when it is lightly toasted & well mixed with the ONION & SALAME, moisten with the WINE, poured a bit at a time, stirring 'til it is completely absorbed.

4) Add a ladleful of the BEANS, VEGETABLES & BROTH, stir 'til the RICE is almost dry, add another ladleful & stir, continuing this process, stirring very often, 'til the RICE is done...about 20 minutes of cooking, depending on how one likes one's rice: it should not get too soft, but remain "AL DENTE", or "biteable".

The PANISCIA may be served immediately but many people take it off the heat just before the RICE is completely cooked & let it sit 5 minutes before eating: in either case, a bit of PEPPER is added when served.

Risotto Alla Piemontese

~ 4 servings ~

The words "ALLA PIEMONTESE" often indicate the presence of truffles & thus this dish is usually rice served with a few slices of this Region's famous white ones. However, considering the rarity & cost of this garnish, it is an optional ingredient & while it certainly adds distinction, this RISOTTO is delicious without it, thanks to the use of homemade beef broth & a few spoonfuls of the Piedmont's inimitable SUGO D'ARROSTO.

2 oz. BUTTER
2 TB. finely chopped ONION
12 oz. ITALIAN RICE, for RISOTTO
½ cup dry WHITE WINE
1 QT. Homemade BEEF BROTH, boiling
3 oz. grated PARMESAN CHEESE
3 TB. SUGO D'ARROSTO (p. 81)

optional WHITE TRUFFLES

1) Melt half the BUTTER in a pot, add the ONION & cook over moderate heat 'til it turns transparent. Add the RICE & cook, stirring, 3-4 minutes. Add the WINE, stirring 'til it has evaporated.

2) Add a ladle of BROTH, stir 'til the mixture becomes "dry"; add another ladleful, stir & continue this process for about 15 minutes. Add half the CHEESE & a dash of SALT & PEPPER (preferably WHITE) & stir gently: the mixture should be creamy.

3) Turn off the heat & cover the pot: after 2-3 minutes the RICE should be chewy, solid but not hard. Add the remaining CHEESE & BUTTER —cut into bits- & mix quickly but gently. Stir in the SUGO D'ARROSTO & serve immediately.

If TRUFFLES are added, they should be sliced razor-thin onto the RISOTTO when it is served.

Rice With Chestnuts   Mach — Machet

~ 4 servings ~

Having read of this rice dish made with milk & chestnuts typical of the Biella area, I had hoped to find this intriguing combination in restaurants but it is now more memory than reality. Young people tend to grimace at the idea of it & older ones admit its particular flavor is not for everyone. Nowadays, chestnuts, & especially the slightly sweeter marrons, are mostly eaten roasted or as an ingredient of certain sweets & are somewhat of a luxury but for centuries they were a fundamental food for mountain dwellers in many parts of Italy –chestnut trees thrive in the Piedmont- & were usually ground for making porridge & polenta.

8 oz. fresh CHESTNUTS *
7 oz. ITALIAN RICE
1 oz. BUTTER
2 cups MILK

1) Shell the NUTS & soak them in tepid water to soften their thin skin so it slips off easily.

2) Put them in a pot with 2 quarts WATER & a pinch of SALT. Boil over medium heat for from 2-2½ hours.

3) Add the RICE & cook 10 minutes. Add the BUTTER & MILK & cook 'til the RICE is done: the MACH should be thick & creamy.

*If dried CHESTNUTS are used, soak them for 10-12 hours in water to cover.

! ADUTA CASTAGNE PERIODO AUTUNNALE

Chestnuts are very present in both rural & urban Piedmont. This unusual sign, CHESTNUTS FALL DURING AUTUMN, is posted on Turin's busy street CORSO RE UMBERTO.

Rice Paste relief decoration on a door in the SALA DELLE TRE FINESTRE (Salon of Three Windows), late 1700's, Castle of Masino (Caravino, Turin). With this humble material anonymous artisans were able to imitate refined works done by famous artists with precious materials. Property of FONDO PER L'AMBIENTE ITALIANO

Piazza Molino,
Agliè

Piazza Molino, or Mill Square, indicates the past presence of a mill, in this case for flour, as does the street on the left, called Via Molino. The tower & wall are part of the **Castello Ducale** in the town of Agliè (Canavese). Built as a fortified castle in the 12th cent., it was transformed into a sumptuous palace in the 1600's. Somewhat destroyed by the French in 1706, it was acquired by the Savoys & later belonged to the Dukes of Genoa. Today it belongs to the State & is open to the public.

Pasta

Stuffed pasta, or PASTA RIPIENA, probably born in central Italy, in Emilia-Romagna, is now eaten throughout the peninsula but is most associated with northern Italy: thin sheets of dough made from the flour of soft wheat –Triticum aestivum-, water and eggs enclose meat, cheese and vegetable fillings giving rise to a seemingly unlimited array of creations that even Italians can find difficult to identify and distinguish. These winsome little squares, circles, half-circles, rings etc. look almost like playthings and even their names are fun to say: AGNOLINI, AGNOLOTTI, ANOLINI, CANNELLONI, CAPPELLETTI, CASONSEI, MARUBINI, RAVIOLI, TORTELLINI, TORTELLONI… are examples of the incredible variety of gastronomic terms used here, where neighbouring towns often call the same food by different names. The diversity of the PASTE RIPIENE lies not only in their form and content but also in whether they are folded over or pressed together, boiled in water or in broth, and how they are eaten, with a fork, in sauce or with a spoon, in broth.

Discussing the origins of pasta and its filling is a bit like asking which came first, the chicken or the egg: they both date back to the remote past but led quite separate lives 'til the 1300's. Pasta was eaten in ancient Italy but most of that culinary culture disappeared with the end of the Roman Empire in the 5th century and many "typical" Italian foods were actually introduced, or reintroduced, here by the Moors starting in the 9th century, such as dried pasta, made from Triticum durum, or hard wheat. They mixed its flour with water, rolled out this dough, cut it into thin strips and dried them in the sun and it is thought that by the year 1000, this PASTA SECCA was known in many parts of Sicily. Nutricious and almost nonperishable, dried pasta withstood the arduous conditions of crossing the desert, endured long sea voyages and proved to be a profitable commmodity of exchange. Hard wheat flourished in Sicily so it was not necessary to import dried pasta: that island, and southern Puglia, had been the Roman Empire's bread basket and it was said that during antiquity so much wheat was harvested there that farmers had trouble storing it. Sicilians were

Treasure Of Marengo
Silver band decorated with embossed spikes of wheat, covered with gold leaf: part of a group of silver objects (1^t cent. B.C.-3rd cent.A.D.), discovered by chance near Alessandria in 1928. Perhaps buried during a period of crisis, they fortunately were not found when Napolean beat the Austrians at Marengo in 1800. The site may have been a center of worship. Museum of Antiquities, Turin

soon producing this food, in the 1200's Genoese merchants were trading it in northern Italy and it soon became a delicacy for the palates of the rich. Pasta is thought to have encouraged the use of forks as an alternative to the hands and anyone who has eaten it that way will no doubt agree. Venetians were the first Europeans to use a fork, introduced to them in the 11th century by the Byzantine princess Teodora, wife of the Doge Michele Steno: one of the refinements of Constantinople's Imperial Court, forks were much critized by the Catholic Church, which was, however, unable to dampen the aristocracy's delight in using them.

Given the omnipresence of pasta today, it is easy to forget that for centuries it was a priority of the rich and privileged; well into the 1800's the wheat that Italian sharecroppers and tenent farmers sowed and reaped was consumed almost entirely by landowners and city dwellers, mostly as bread. For centuries, white flour was as expensive as meat and the bread made from it was a luxury, as was pasta: the art of pasta making was laborious and time-consuming, requiring physical force and skills acquired through long experience, which added to its cost. Reserved for special occasions, it was usually served to impress one's guests, as a symbol of affluence, and until the 1700's was seasoned with precious spices, like cinnamon and sugar, and grated cheese.

Triticum, both hard and soft, is the most prized member of the large Graminaceae family. It contains two proteins that not only make it more nutricious than other grains but which also have unique properties: gliadin is sticky and soft while glutenin, rich in amino acids, is tough and elastic and when wheat kernels are ground into flour and this is mixed with water, the two proteins unite to form a single, very strong, flexible, springy one called gluten which makes dough kneadable and lets it expand, rise and be rolled without cracking. Without Triticum's gluten, pasta and most bread would not exist. Wheat's qualities had long been exploited but they were not scientifically understood 'til Jacopo Bartolomeo Beccari (1682-1766), from Bologona, professor of physics, chemistry and logic, studied it and discovered the glutenous and starchy substances in its flour.

While some Italians were enjoying dried pasta, people were also eating rissole-like balls, or RAVIOLI, a word perhaps derived from one of their main ingredients, RAVVIGIOLO, a ricotta-type cheese from the Apennines in Tuscany and Romagna, or from RAPA, or turnip, once an extremely common

Wheat, from marble altar in the Collegiate Church of San Secondo, Asti

73

food here. Rissoles are made all over the world and can consist of almost anything, from stale bread to vegetables to legumes to meat, mashed or minced and bound with eggs or milk. Although it is said that such balls were born to put leftovers to good use, poor people rarely had enough to eat in the first place, to say nothing of leftovers and the rich could afford fresh food every day, as well as choice RAVIOLI which, in fact, were prized morsels for them. Flavored with exotic spices, they were classified as MAGRI (thin), made with cheese or vegetables, GRASSI (fat), made with meat, fowl or sausage and DOLCI (sweet), made with sugar and crushed almonds. Originally fried in suet, by the mid-1400's they were also being cooked in broth or water and seasond, like pasta, with cinnamon, sugar and grated cheese. Already very tasty, these little tidbits were to reach new heights as they became intimately combined with pasta: in the words of food historians, naked, "undressed" RAVIOLI NUDI were "clothed", wrapped with a thin piece of dough. The union between the two, however, (as with many profound relationships) came about gradually and, at first, although cooked together, they remained quite independent. They were called TORTE, a name thought to derive, again, from their main ingredients, cooked vegetables, which, to eliminate their moisture, were TORTE, or wrung, twisted, "tortured", from the past tense of the verb TORCERE.

TORTE consisted of a filling and dough but the latter was a very thick crust that served to hold and support the former, functioning as a container-cooking vessel and was not eaten, being too hard and tough to chew. Baked in an oven, or since ovens were scarce, in a fireplace surrounded by hot embers, stones or specially-made clay tiles, the TORTE, also called PASTICCI, were made with all sorts of fillings, from humble and simple to rich and elaborate. Once baked, they could be transported and eaten virtually anywhere: medieval merchants and religious pilgrims took them on their travels, as described by the 13th century monk Salimbene da Parma in his "Cronaco" (chronicle), in which he recorded details about social customs, politics, agriculture, weather, epidemics, foods, etc. as he journeyed through central and northern Italy. The Piedmont's geographic position made it the overland link between Western Europe and the rest of the peninsula: a myriad of roads crossed it, the most famous being the VIA FRANCIGENA, on the pilgrimage route that went from Canterbury to

Rome. The TORTE that people carried were usually homemade but could be acquired ready to eat; it was also possible to prepare the ingredients at home and bring them to a baker for baking, a service that bakers in Ivrea, an important point on the FRANCIGENA, had to offer free to regular customers. CROSTATE, from CROSTA, or crust, were baked like the TORTE, the difference being in the filling's consistency: the CROSTATA contained large pieces of meat or vegetables while the TORTA'S ingredients were more homogeneous. During the 1400's the tough "baking-pan" exterior of these pies became increasingly tender as lard, butter and /or eggs were mixed with the flour and ceramic and iron containers replaced the thick crust. This softer, more pliable dough offered new creative possibilities and perhaps in an effort to amuse their noble, or merely wealthy, employers, chefs started making little individual TORTE, or TORTELLINI. Today, TORTE may be sweet or "salted", a cake or a meat-cheese-vegetable pie but CROSTATE are only desserts. PASTICCIO is a casserole of meat, cheese, vegetables or fish, topped with a layer of pasta: its seemingly disordered composition explains why PASTICCIO also means a tricky, confusing, difficult situation. These culinary developments, perfected by talented cooks, also owed a great deal to agricultural progress that improved the quality and quantity of certain crops.

In the 9th century harnesses for horses, rigid padded collars that rest on their shoulders, began to be used instead of the bovine yokes that obstructed their breathing and could strangle them when pulled hard, and iron shoes were invented to protect their hoofs. The discovery of new iron mines and the growing expertise of blacksmiths led to better and stronger tools and utensils, especially important for plows' cutting blades: during the late Middle Ages the Pied-

75

mont boasted some of Europe's largest, most
Region's future industrial eminence. Oxen,
ian, and Mediterranean, agriculture:
but they cost more to feed and oats,
mild climate. Changes in the
probably born from a stick
shaped bough, were
The heavy   plow, devised in
and compact,   introduced here by
the plain's rich,   clayey earth
used for the Mediter-   ranean world's
not turned over in or-
ing. It is said that the
and the landscape it tilled.
one: it had more metal parts,
many as four pairs of animals to
steer it. Farmers began to pool their
birth to the concept of a cooperative, and
the pairs of beasts one behind the other,
and fields became more rectangular than
with its relatively great expanse of flat land,
ments in spite of this plain's being a quite unu-
raphy of which 70% is mountains
43% mountains and 32% hills and
stricted to small, irregular plots, often
and sometimes too steep for animals.
However, the limitations that this terrain imposes are frequently responsible
for the pleasing, picturesque patterns and
shapes that characterize much of Italy's beautiful countryside... more efficient equipment often
means less aesthetics.

Of great consequence for wheat was another
major medieval achievement: the exploiting of hy-

productive forges, as if a prophetic sign of this
however, continued to be protagonists in Ital-
horses walk faster and have more endurance
their favorite food, do not grow well in Italy's
plow; the primordial agrarian instrument
dragged along the ground, replaced by a Y-
particularly relevant for the Po River Plain.
northern Europe where the soil is damp
northern invaders, was better for working
than the light, symetric scratch plow
powdery, dry soil which is broken but
der to keep its moisture from evaporat-
heavy plow also affected social relations
It was more expensive than the light
metal was costly, and it required as
pull it and more than one person to
resources and work together, giving
as this plow was very long, due to
turning it was rather complicated
square. The PIANURA PADANA,
benefitted from these develop-
sual feature of Italy's topog-
or hills: the Piedmont is
much farming is re-
difficult to plow

sloira, or plow: wood & iron, 19th cent. Museum of
Historic Trades, Cisterna d'Asti

draulic energy to turn mills, a resource virtually ignored by the ancient Romans whose grinding stones were rotated by slaves or animals. Problems posed by the scarcity, or total lack, of water in many Italian rivers during certain months —but they rarely freeze- were often remedied by building dams, locks and canals and by the 13th century thousands of flour, textile, saw and paper mills were operating across Italy as elsewhere in Europe. Massive stones tuned by vertical and horizontal wooden wheels were efficient as never before. This natural energy functioned 24 hours a day without need of being fed, like people and animals, and more of the grain's components could be ground, and more finely, than previously. In spite of the difficulty of transporting hard, weighty stone from mountain quarries it was a very profitable object of commerce, controlled by the cities of Ivrea and Vercelli from the 1200's. The great cost of building mills meant that, at first, only feudal lords and large religious institions could afford them, and they usually also held the rights to the waters that propelled them. But, as urban communities became more independent and autonomous, city authorities began to take over this lucrative activity; fixed and floating mills were soon operating, such as those along Turin's two rivers,

Gros Passet, *Val Germanasca. One of several historic water mills in this remote mountain valley where, in 1100, the Waldenses found refuge from religious persecution. The mills ground wheat, rye, barley, buckwheat, chestnuts & dried beans. A scenic hiking path links the mills & includes other points of interest. This area is still inhabited by descendents of the original settlers.*

and municipal ovens were opened nearby, coveted signs of a community's prosperity and importance.

Millers had to master a wide range of skills: they had to know how to choose appropriate stones and carve them, to control the water's flow so as to insure the wheel's regular, constant turning, to understand how different types of wood resist water, to repair faulty parts, to evaluate a grain's potential yield in flour. In short, every aspect of the mill depended on their prowess. Not surprisingly, they played a fundamental, sometimes controversial, role, for disagreements over the weight of sacks of grain and the flour they produced were common, and since a percentage of everything they ground went to municipal treasuries, they were often accused of fraud. In fact, it was often asserted that a miller's honesty was even more important than his excellence. Mills also had a social function. They were an informal but fixed place to meet, wait and carry out other activities as evidenced by the fact that clerics frequently tried to eliminate the numerous prostitutes who gathered there, attracted by the men who came to grind, buy or sell wheat and flour.

Where water flow was continuous, as along the Po River, mills with paddle wheels were installed that could be moved to exploit changes in the current but where it was seasonal, as with rushing mountain torrents so common in Italy, the water was collected and stored in a sort of large basin and powered mills through a delicate system of locks that functioned only at certain times of the year, depending on rainfall and melting snow. The mechanisn of these early water wheels served as models for more advanced and complicated gear devices and many mills continued to operate well after steam engines were invented; some were still grinding in the early 20th century and though now replaced by other forms of energy, the word MOLINO, or mill, found in many place names, is a reminder of their past life.

Although the agricultural innovations of the Middle Ages and the Renaissance continued to evolve with varying intensity over the following

Hoes from "Manuale dell'Ortolano contenente la coltivazione ordinaria e forzata delle piante d'ortaggio"(manual regarding cultivation of vegetables, their normal & precocious growth) by the Rodi Brothers, printed in Turin, 1892 (3rd ed.) Each hoe is suited for a particular task: squarish for loose, plowed soil; pointed for removing stones & roots etc. The manual also recommends shorter handles in mountainous areas & on inclined land than for flat terrain. It was said that few farmers used the hoe as skillfully as the Piedmontese. La Vigna Library, Vicenza

centuries, no significant changes occurred in Italy until the mid-1800's when new plows, based on Belgian, English and French examples were introduced into Tuscany and then spread to other regions: by perfecting the curve of their iron moldboards, for instance, a more efficient angle of traction was obtained. However, it was the slow and diffident acceptance of motorized machines that truly revolutionized farming, the most important probably being the steam-powered thresher which not only liberated farm workers from one of their most exhausting tasks, carried out during the hottest part of the summer, but it also helped make pasta more accessible to them. Until the 19th century, the husk of wheat, and other grains, was removed by repeatedly beating the spikes with a CORREGIATO, or flail, and sometimes horses would tread over them to split them open. They were further cleaned by being tossed up into the air and caught with large sieves, a much trickier operation than it may seem. Thus, it is not surprising that pasta was a precious commodity and to this day, the freshly-made version remains a special food. The Piedmont's two characteristic types, both made with egg dough, are from the Langhe area: TAJARIN are noodles and AGNOLOTTI are stuffed.

Castle Falletti di Barolo, Serralunga d'Alba (Langhe) Built before the 1300's, when it was restructured, its extreme verticality makes it unique among the Piedmont's many castles. Its form, combined with its position on the top of a hill (414 mt.) made it an important bastion of observation & defense. Recently restored, it belongs to the State & is open to the public.

79

Tajarin

TAJARIN is Piedmontese for TAGLIA-TELLE, from the verb TAGLIARE, to cut. They are thin egg noodles, usually served with SUGO D'ARROSTO, the strained cooking juices of veal rump cooked slowly with little liquid. Other Italians often describe the PIEMONTESI as having a BASSO PROFILO, or low-profile, and TAJARIN AL SUGO D'ARROSTO is a culinary example of this tendency to let the quality of something speak for itself without frills or spectacle. The bowl of steaming noodles with the roasting juices has neither the brilliant color of sauces like tomato or PESTO nor the visual interest of those made from seafood, mushrooms or certain vegetables. In fact, it looks rather plain. But, what appears to be a nondescript brownish accompaniment to the pasta is actually a richly flavored blend of ingredients and a bit of this incredible SUGO gives character to a variety of other dishes. TAJARIN are also eaten with butter melted with fresh sage leaves. Some restaurants offer them with tomato sauce, a concession to tourism: locals feel that condiment is meant for spaghetti.

There is a rule for the width of TAJARIN, from two to three millimeters (c. 1/8 inch), but some leeway regarding their limited ingredients, determined by local customs, personal preference and their sauce. Some people use one egg for every 200 grams (7 ounces) of flour, others, mostly in the province of Alba, use two. A bit of yellow-corn flour is sometimes added to the soft wheat flour, especially if eaten with a chicken liver sauce; other optionals are a spoonful of olive oil, white wine, tepid water or grated parmesan cheese. A pinch of salt is usual but not necssary. It would be presumptuous to expect to make perfect TAJARIN immediately; the art of making pasta by hand requires practice and patience. Italians prepare this dough on a flat surface but if the thought of eggs spreading uncontrollably through the flour is frightening, a wide bowl can be used.

Grain Kiosk, 15th cent., Dronero Valle Maira This LOGGIA de GRANO was built for gra market negotiations. After a plague 1522 ... arc wer wal & it becar a chapel; a baroque entrance & clock were added in the 1700's & in th 1800's it was again used for co merce. Dronero produces an extraordinary sweet, called DRUNE: cho late-rum between meringue wafers.

Tajarin

These thin egg noodles are normally served with
SUGO D'ARROSTO or butter melted with fresh
sage leaves. In the Langhe, where filbert trees are
cultivated (p. 139-142), they are sometimes
topped with this nut, very finely chopped.

14 oz. FLOUR
2-4 EGGS (some people prefer those with dark
shells as their yolks are often more yellow)
3-4 TB. WATER or 2 TB. OLIVE OIL

When making the PASTA be sure there are no
strong air currents which could make it too dry. On
a flat surface, or in a very wide bowl, form the
FLOUR into a ring. Work the EGGS & WATER into
the FLOUR: either put them directly in the center or
lightly beat them in a bowl & then add them, mixing them with the fingertips, not with a fork.
Knead the dough energetically for 10-15 minutes: it
should become firm, smooth & elastic. Form it into
a ball & flatten with the palms of the hands. Sprinkle a bit of flour on a flat surface & roll out the
dough, very thin, moving a long, slim rolling pin
with the palms. If the dough seems too moist, dust
it with flour: sticky dough is hard to manipulate.

With a very sharp knife, cut the dough into
strips about 3mm. wide (1/8 inch). The slight irregularity of their handcut width is a prized feature, as opposed to mechanical perfection. Let them
sit about 5 minutes to dry a bit. Carefully drop the
TAJARIN into about 2 quarts of briskly boiling
salted water & boil 3-4 minutes, then drain. Serve
immediately with hot SUGO D'ARROSTO. Grated
PARMESAN CHEESE is served separately.

Sugo d'Arrosto

2 lb. Piece of VEAL – top round or rolled, boned
shoulder
1 clove GARLIC, cut into slivers
sprig of ROSEMARY
1-1 ½ oz. BUTTER
1-1 ½ oz. PANCETTA (unsmoked bacon) or
LARD, minced
2 cups homemade BEEF BROTH
1 TB. TOMATO SAUCE or PASTE

1. Cut tiny slits in the VEAL & insert the
GARLIC & ROSEMARY leaves.

2. Melt the BUTTER with the PANCETTA
or LARD in the pot the VEAL will be cooked in.
Add the MEAT & lightly brown it, turning it to
color all over.

3. Mix the TOMATO, with a pinch of SALT
& PEPPER, into the BROTH & add a ladleful to
the MEAT. Cover & cook slowly 1 ½ - 2 hours, occasionally adding a spoonful of BROTH.

4. Set the MEAT aside: it can be used for
stuffing AGNOLOTTI or vegetables or served as a
second course. Strain the cooking juices, which
are used to season TAJARIN or AGNOLOTTI or to
enrich the flavor of other dishes.

Seminatrice... machine for sowing wheat Engraving from
"Trattato della Seminazione de'Campi e della Coltivazione
de'Prati" (on sowing & cultivating) by Giambattista Ratti,
published in Casale Monferrato in 1764. Born in Massiola
(Valstrona), Ratti (1680-1766) moved to Casale where, with
his earnings as an ironmonger, he bought land & devoted
himself to agriculture &, with his son's collaboration, to creating farm machines & perfecting existing implements. The
advantages of the SEMINATRICE over manual
sowing were great: it was more efficient
(50% of hand sowed seeds were
wasted) & seeds were
more evenly distrib-
uted & went deeper
into the soil. Ratti
father & son
studied new
agrarian tech-
niques underway
in other
countries
& helped modernize
Italian farming in the 18th
cent. La Vigna Library, Vicenza.

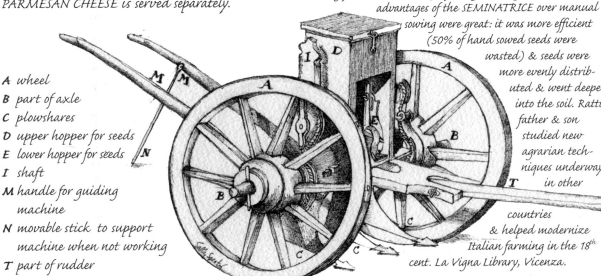

A wheel
B part of axle
C plowshares
D upper hopper for seeds
E lower hopper for seeds
I shaft
M handle for guiding
    machine
N movable stick to support
    machine when not working
T part of rudder

Agnolotti

Although AGNOLOTTI, also called RAVIOLI, are eaten in many parts of Italy, they are typically Piedmontese and began to be described as such in cookbooks in the 1800's. It is generally thought that the word AGNOLOTTO derives from AGNELLO, or lamb, perhaps once used for the filling, though no trace of this ingredient appears in printed recipes, past or present. ANELLO, or ring, is also suggested as an etymological source, implying their form was circular, and not square, as nowadays. Their dimensions and filling vary, depending on the season, local products and the whims of the cook and every city, town and family has its own AGNOLOTTO. The classic version is stuffed with meat, usually a mixture of veal and pork but chicken, rabbit, quail, donkey or horsemeat may be used, along with a bit of fresh sausage, veal brains and a vegetable such as cabbage, plus eggs, grated cheese and nutmeg; vegetables and cheese, if desired, may replace the meat. Stuffed pasta is usually made by first cutting the little shapes, then a dab of filling is placed on half of it, the dough is folded over and the edges pressed together. AGNOLOTTI, instead, are prepared by placing spoonfuls of filling along a strip of dough which is then covered with another strip, the area around each little mound is pressed with the fingers and little squares are cut with a toothed roller, never a smooth blade. A unique variation of the AGNOLOTTO PIEMONTESE is the AGNOLOT COL PLIN or " with a pinch": an expert combination of a twist and a squeeze gives them their distinguishing touch and the tinier they are, the more they are prized. It would be unrealistic to try and make them without guidance: fortunately, they are found in restaurants and fresh pasta shops. The words AGNOLOTTI and RAVIOLI are used interchangeably.

In the Langhe and the Monferrato areas AGNOLOTTI used to be eaten without condiment. Tied together in a cloth, they were immersed into a pot of boiling liquid: kept hot constantly, it was never emptied, which would have been wasteful. Brought directly to the table, they were served directly from the cloth, felt to be the best way of savoring the perfect equilibrium of their ingredients and the thinness of their dough. Today, AGNOLOTTI, like TAJARIN, are servd with SUGO D'ARROSTO or butter melted with fresh sage leaves, then sprinkled with grated cheese. Tomato and cream sauces are considered unsuitable.

In the past, the filling for AGNOLOTTI consisted of whatever leftovers happened to be available & since virtually anything edible fell into this category, it often included bits & pieces not particularly tempting on their own. It is thus easy to understand why there was no single, classic recipe but, rather, constantly changing renditions of this dish. Thanks to improved standards of living today's version is ennobled by the use of quality ingredients, choice cuts of meat & fresh vegetables. Until quite recently AGNOLOTTI were a special-occasion dish, eaten to celebrate Christmas, weddings, baptisms etc.: for many people that connotation remains 'tho they are more common now than in the past. Many fresh pasta & some butcher shops offer them with a variety of fillings & due to their nutricious interior, they sometimes substitute for the traditional meat course of family meals. Making them is a challenge but even first attempts can be satisfying.

Agnolotti from the MERCATO COPERTO (covered market), Asti

Pasta Dough:

14 oz. FLOUR

2 or more EGGS

1-2 TB. WATER or OLIVE OIL

    Follow the directions for making TAJARIN (p.81). When the dough is firm & elastic form it into a ball, wrap in a cotton cloth & let sit at room temperature 30 minutes. Prepare the filling.

Meat Filling:

1 oz. BUTTER

3 TB. SUGO D'ARROSTO (p.81)

2 oz. fresh SAUSAGE, skinned & finely chopped

3 oz. SAVOY CABBAGE or ESCAROLE, finely chopped

7 oz. cooked BEEF, finely chopped*

3 oz. cooked PORK, finely chopped

1 EGG

2 TB. grated PARMESAN CHEESE

grated NUTMEG

optional 2 oz. VEAL BRAINS, boiled & chopped

*or equal amounts of cooked CHICKEN, RABBIT, QUAIL etc., finely chopped

    1. Melt the BUTTER in a heavy pot over moderate heat, add the SUGO D'ARROSTO, SAUSAGE & CABBAGE or ESCAROLE & cook 6-7 minutes. Stir almost constantly & if necessary, moisten with a bit of water. Let cool. Add the MEAT & optional BRAINS to the pot & mix well. Add the EGG, CHEESE & a pinch of NUTMEG, SALT & PEPPER & mix well.

    2. Roll the dough out, very thin, into a rectangle & cut it into two equal strips. Cover one with the cloth, on the other, place spoonfuls of the filling at regularly spaced intervals, about 1 ½ inches apart: do not use a pastry tube as it alters the fill-

Pepper from Kenya

ing's consistency. Cover it with the other sheet of dough & with the fingers, press gently around each little mound. With a toothed roller, not a smooth blade, cut square AGNOLOTTI. They can be cooked immediately or set aside a couple of hours on a cloth dusted with flour.

    3. Drop the AGNOLOTTI into a large pot of rapidly boiling salted water or BEEF BROTH. Boil them 3-5 minutes: time depends on the dough's thickness. When they rise to the surface check for doneness & remove with a slotted spoon. Serve immediately with hot SUGO D'ARROSTO, with BUTTER melted with fresh SAGE leaves or in a bowl with the BEEF BROTH. Serve grated PARMESAN CHEESE separately.

Cheese Filling:

14 oz. CHEESE: use a mixture of hard ones that melt well, cut in slivers or grated (FONTINA, TOMA etc.) or soft ones (GORGONZOLA, RICOTTA)

2 EGG YOLKS

1 ½ TB. fresh minced PARSLEY

3 ½ oz. grated PARMESAN CHEESE

dash of BLACK PEPPER & grated NUTMEG

    Combine all the ingredients & mix well 'til thick & creamy. Prepare the AGNOLOTTI & fill them, as above, with the CHEESE mixture. Boil in salted water & when they rise to the surface, remove them. Serve with BUTTER melted with fresh SAGE leaves.

    Practice is necesary for making AGNOLOTTI, as for all fresh pasta, but one should not feel intimidated. It would be pretentious, however, to think that AGNOLOT COL PLIN are similarly feasible. Once they were made only south of the River Tanaro but today are found in much of the Piedmont.

Zangola, or BUTTER CHURN, 15th cent., from Valle Maira. Museum of the City of Cuneo

Gnocchi

Gnocchi, little dumplings, are eaten in many parts of Itay. Their name derives from KNOHHA, the Lombard word for knot & knuckle, which became KNOKLE in Low German. In fact, GNOCCHI more closely resemble a knuckle than the ball-like dumplings of Northern Europe & the term is also used for a small form of pasta. Originally made from flour & water, in the late 1700's mashed potatoes began to be added to the dough: this tuber was introduced into Italy in the late 1500's but was long considered a food for animals, not humans. Its unprepossessing appearance & the fact that it grows underground, in the dark, made it an object of suspect but it is also possible that Italy's mild climate & fertile terrain which nurture a plentitute of vegetables made it less necessary a crop than in colder countries where cultivation is more limited. GNOCCHI PIEMONTESI are usually made with cheese, as in the recipes below, & served with butter melted with fresh sage leaves.

Butter Stamp,
19th cent., carved
from pine wood.
Collection of Domenico Musci,
Caselle Torinese, Torino

Gnocchi With Ricotta

2 LB. POTATOES
7 oz. FLOUR
7 oz. fresh RICOTTA if possible, from sheep's milk. Remove moisture by draining or patting with paper towels.
2-3 TB. grated PARMESAN CHEESE

Boil, peel & mash the POTATOES. When a bit cooled, stir in the CHEESES, a dash of SALT & a bit at a time, the FLOUR. When the mixture has a uniform consistency, make the GNOCCHI as for the BASIC RECIPE. Serve with BUTTTER melted with fresh SAGE leaves.

Basic Recipe
~ · 4 servings · ~

2 LB. POTATOES (floury ones are best)
7 oz. FLOUR

Wash the POTATOES, put them in a pot of salted water to cover & boil, covered, 'til soft. Drain & peel them immediately: their skin slips off easily in cool water. Mash them while still hot & work in the flour in small amounts 'til the mixture has a uniform consistency & does not stick to the hands. On a flat surface, dusted with flour, form the dough into thin sticks, cut these in pieces about ¾ inch long & flatten them a bit by pressing gently with the prongs of a fork. Drop them into a deep pot of boiling salted water; when they rise to the surface, the sign they are done, remove with a slotted spoon. Serve immediately with hot SUGO D'ARROSTO (p. 81) or with BUTTER melted with fresh SAGE leaves.

Gnocchi Alla Bava

literally, "dribbling, drooling dumplings": BAVA
refers to the way the melted cheese "drools " over &
around the GNOCCHI

Prepare the BASIC RECIPE
5 oz. CHEESE: TOMA, FONTINA or other good
melting cheese, cut into bits
3 oz. BUTTER

Preheat oven to 475°. Make the GNOCCHI,
cook & drain them. In a buttered baking container arrange them in alternating layers with
the CHEESE. Dot with BUTTER, cover & bake
about 5 minutes. Serve immediately.

Raviolas
GNOCCHI of the Valle Varaita

2 LB. POTATOES
¾ LB. TOMA or
other good melting
CHEESE, cut in bits
1 EGG
1 TB. OLIVE OIL
7-8 oz. FLOUR
2 oz. heavy CREAM
4 oz. BUTTER

Variation
While preparing the potato purée is relatively
easy, forming the individual GNOCCHI can be less
so. Thus, this variation, in which they are
dropped by spoonfuls into the boiling water is particularly inviting & visually interesting as well.

1 ¾ LB. POTATOES
3 EGGS, separated
5 oz. FLOUR
WHITE PEPPER freshly grated
NUTMEG
4 TB. grated PARMESAN CHEESE

Boil, peel & mash the POTATOES. In
a bowl, beat the EGG WHITES 'til
stiff, add the YOLKS, FLOUR,
dash of NUTMEG, SALT
& PEPPER & gently
stir in the PO-
TATOES.

Boil, peel & mash the POTATOES. Stir in the
CHEESE & form the mixture into a circle on a flat
surface. Put the EGG & OIL in the center & mix
into the dough. Add the FLOUR slowly, work to a
firm consistency & spread into a flat rectangle.
Cut strips 1 1/8 inches wide, roll these into sticks
& cut into pieces 2 inches long. Form the
RAVIOLAS into spindle-like shapes with a slight
S-curve. Dust them with flour & drop into a deep
pot of boiling water. When they rise to the surface,
remove & serve immediately with the CREAM &
BUTTER, heated together.

Bring a deep
pot salted water to
a boil: drop spoonfuls of
the mixture into the pot &
when they rise to the surface, remove
with a slotted spoon & place on a heated platter.
Sprinkle with the grated CHEESE & serve immediately with BUTTER melted with fresh SAGE
leaves.

Polenta Concia

POLENTA is one of Italy's most historic dishes: since the remote past people have prepared a sort of porridge of ground grain mixed with water. In Italy, barley, millet and FARRO, or emmer wheat, were most often used before corn was introduced into Europe after Columbus discovered the New World. Starting in the 1500's, this plant brought numerous changes to agriculture in northern and central Italy and for centuries provided nourishment for millions of people here who ate cornmeal POLENTA every day, twice a day, often flavored only by rubbing a slice of it against a communal salted anchovy.

Though wheat is more nutricious, corn has higher yields, is easier to grow and prospers even on hilly terrain: by the 1600's it had all but replaced a variety of inferior grains —millet, foxtail millet, sorghum, spelt, rye- that one thousand years earlier had replaced the wheat that Etruscans and Romans had cultivated across the Po River Plain. Long considered a "poor person's food" here, POLENTA was disdained as standards of living and diets improved in the 1900's. Today, fortunately, Italians eat it by choice, not out of necessity, and in the Piedmont it is usually enhanced by the addition of excellent local cheese and butter.

Today in the Piedmont there is a new appreciation of stone grinding which breaks the kernels without squashing them as happens with the metal cylinders used in industrial mills. Varieties of corn grown here in the past are reputed to have been more flavorable than the larger, softer kernels of today's hybrids and there is new interest in returning to the smaller, harder ones that produce a coarser but much creamier POLENTA. They are also well suited for making the Piedmont's famous cornmeal cookies, PASTE DI MELIGA (p. 153, 155).

In spite of its associations with the lower class, POLENTA is included in Giovanni Vialardi's book "Trattato di cucina pasticcera moderna, credenza e relativa confetturia" published in 1854. Chef for the royal House of Savoy during the second half of the 1800's, his book was written for the comfortable middle class & a recipe for POLENTA is suitably enriched: the POLENTA is cooked in broth & at the last minute, grated cheese & butter are added along with thinly sliced truffles.

One of the most delicious ways of eating cornmeal is POLENTA CONCIA, or POLENTA CONDITA, that is, "seasoned", typical of the area of Biella.

~ 4 servings ~

3 cups MILK, 3 cups WATER, 11 oz. CORNMEAL
5 oz. each TOMA & FONTINA CHEESE, cut into cubes or thin strips
4 oz. BUTTER
4-5 TB. grated PARMESAN CHEESE

1) Bring the MILK & WATER to a boil in a large pot. Slowly add the CORNMEAL, pouring it in a continuous stream. Lower the heat a bit & with a wooden spoon stir constantly about 45 minutes. The mixture should be smooth & creamy & will begin to pull away from the side of the pot. Add the CHEESE & continue cooking & stirring for 15-20 minutes.

2)Heat the BUTTER in a saucepan 'til it turns a warm, nut-brown color. Pour the POLENTA into a serving bowl, or individual ones, sprinkle with PARMESAN CHEESE, pour on the BUTTER & serve immediately.

Variation: Instead of mixing the POLENTA & CHEESE together, they can be treated as for GNOCCHI ALLA BAVA (p. 85). Cook the POLENTA, stirring constantly, about one hour. Pour a thin layer of it in an ovenproof container, cover this with a layer of CHEESE & continue alternating them, finishing with a topping of CHEESE. Bake briefly in a hot oven 'til the CHEESE has completely melted.

Polenta with Leek Sauce

12 oz. coarse Corn Meal
1 ½ TB. BUTTER
12 oz. white part of LEEKS, cut into thin circles & rinsed
1 cup CREAM
4-5 TB. MILK

1) Bring 1 ½ quarts of salted WATER to boiling & add the CORN MEAL: it must be poured slowly & continuously, "A PIOGGIA" –like rain falling- as the Italians say. Lower the heat a bit & cook, stirring very often, for at least 45 minutes.

2) Heat the BUTTER, add the LEEKS & cook them over low heat 'til soft & wilted. Add a pinch of SALT & PEPPER, the CREAM & MILK & cook 20-25 minutes.

3) Spoon the POLENTA into soup bowls & serve the sauce separately.

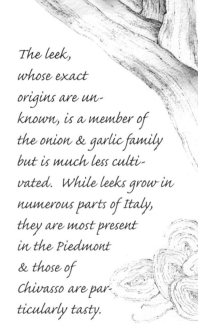

The leek, whose exact origins are unknown, is a member of the onion & garlic family but is much less cultivated. While leeks grow in numerous parts of Italy, they are most present in the Piedmont & those of Chivasso are particularly tasty.

Soups   Zuppe

$\mathcal{V}$isitors to Italy are often surprized by the scarcity of
soups on restaurant menus and even in home cook-
ing they have been much replaced by pasta but every part of the
peninsula has several distinctive, typical ZUPPE. The term soup
derives from the Indo-European SEUK, meaning damp and juice,
the Latin sucus, or juice, and sugere, to suck and from the German SUPPA, which is a moistened piece of bread, a food intimately connected with soup. Since the remote past, the great
majority of Italy's, and Europe's, population ate mostly cereals
—millet, foxtail millet, rye, sorghum and wheat- which in periods
of famine (which were frequent) were supplemented with, or substi-
tuted by, chestnuts, acorns and even nut shells. These were normally
ground into meal to make bread which was usually so hard or stale
it had to be moistened in order to eat it and PANE BAGNATO, or
dampened bread, was synonymous for soup. The phrase, SE NON E'
ZUPPA E' PANE BAGNATO (if it isn't soup it's wet bread) makes
clear the fundamental relationship between this dish and its
contents, vestiges of which remain in traditional recipes that,
thanks to improved standards of living, have been enriched with
additional ingredients. While today the Piedmontese normally
start a meal with antipasti, in the past, they began with soup.

Vegetables such as onions, cabbage and turnips and herbs, usually parsley, sage, and rosemary (in the Piedmont, carrots, basil and
marjoram were used for medicinal purposes during the Middle Ages and the Renaissance)
greatly improved early soups, not only for their nutritional value but also for flavor: salt was
expensive and used sparingly, spices were an imported luxury reserved for the rich and the
bread described above was often decidedly unappetizing. Italy's preponderance of hills and
mountains makes farming difficult or impossible in many places but the mild climate here
permits a long growing season —sometimes two harvests a year- and the fertile soil yields extremely tasty crops and in the Piedmont, for example, the disadvantages of cold winters are
normally compensated for by suffucient rain during the summer. Thus, people here have
been able to enjoy a rich supply and variety of vegetables. Foreigners have long marveled at

Open Market,
Piazza Marco
Alessandria

the beauty of this product while Italians living abroad often wrote of their longing for certain fruits and greens not available in other countries. Italians, in fact, were nicknamed MANGIAFOGLIE, or "leaf-eaters" by the meat-eaters of much of the rest of Europe and vegetables are still a unifying feature of the peninsula's cuisine. ORTAGGI, or vegetables, from the Latin hortu, meaning an enclosed, walled area, were probably the most democratic forms of nourishment when diet was greatly determined by social class. By the late Middle Ages, except for a bit of pork sausage, meat had virtually disappeared from poor people's tables for game, along with freshwater fish, had become an exclusive right of the wealthy and titled but everyone in Italy ate some kinds of vegetables, differences being in how they were eaten, whether as a side dish ennobled with spices and raisins to accompany roast meat or, instead, as the main component of a drab, watery soup.

For centuries, vegetable gardens were part of both urban and rural life in the Piedmont: city and town residents often had a small plot of land or part of a courtyard attached to their dwelling or on the community's periphery, preferably near a river, which supplied food for private cosumption. Sometimes laws were passed requiring every family to grow enough ORTAGGI to fulfill its needs and any surplus could be sold at local markets, offering women one of the few chances they had to work outside the home and this product could even be traded on holidays, perhaps because perishable. The value of these gardens, or

ORTI, is seen in the fact that they normally were surrounded by brick or stone walls with locked entries and medieval registers frequently list fines imposed for abusive entry and theft of crops, sovereign among them being cabbage and turnips, respectively the King and Queen of ORTAGGI until the 1700's.

Etymologists asertain that the word turnip is not related to any other term in any other language: it probably derives from the French TOUR or the English turn, in the sense of round, thus referring to its shape, and from the Middle English NEPE, from napus, the Latin name for the rape, a European mustard plant and close relative of the turnip. Both the rape and turnip are called RAPA in Italian and have been harvested, like cabbage, since the remote past, their domestication perhaps facilitated by the fact that these root vegetables often grow wild among cultivated crops. Turnips were of primary importance in the diet of ancient Romans: in his "Natural History", Pliny wrote of various types found in northern Italy and particularly in Gaul, now France, where well into the 1800's they were still highly valued, especially during the winter for their resistence to cold. The rutabaga, for example, from the Swedish dialect word ROTABAGGE, is a yellow turnip of Mediterranean origin, as are all turnips, introduced first into Scotland in the 1700's and then into Scandinavia where it adapted and now thrives. It is said that the flavor of turnips improves with the advent of chilly weather, held to be true for other vegetables. Best cooked in rich beef broth, during the Middle Ages it was believed that, with the addition of herbs and pepper, this dish would excite and stimulate young men for the "battles of Venus". It also had very concrete benefits for the RAPA played a major role in improving medieval farming: sowed with cereals and clover, it greatly enriched a soil's fertility, making crops stronger and less vulnerable to disease and it hindered the growth of weeds, of much importance as the best fertilizer, manure, was always scarce and insecticides and herbicides were not introduced 'til the 1900's. Until quite recently a common ingredient of soups, today the consumption of turnips is far less –a shame, for they are delicious- but they are more present in the Piedmont than other parts of Italy.

The numerous species and varieties of cabbage, or CAVOLO, their ability to withstand cold temperatures, their remarkable capacity to adapt to diverse growing situations and conditions - they are harvested in every season- and their fecundity puts them among the most generous of edible plants. Thus it is not surprising that they are often considered humanity's most important vegetable. The most com-

Detail from *"View of Old Bridge over the Po River"*, oil on canvas by Bernardo Bellotto(1721-1780), painted for Carlo Emanuele III, King of Sardinia, in 1745. Pinacoteca Sabauda, Turin.

mon cabbages in Italy are the Brassica oleracea Sabauda, or Savoy cabbage, usually called VERZA, and the Brassica oleracea capitola, called CAPPUCCIO. The name VERZA presumably derives from the Latin viridia, meaning green, for it presents a stunning range of shades of this color, often with touches of violet on its outer, "bumpy" leaves that surround the head quite loosely, like flower petals. CAPPUCCIO, or hood, from the Latin cappa, is pale green, almost white, its smooth leaves closed tightly around its ball-like shape. An extraordinary example of the VERZA grows around Montaldo Dora, in the Canavese, this town being long renowned for its winter cabbage crop thanks to deposits left by ancient glaciers and by the Dora Baltea River which make the soil there very fertile. With the first frost, usually in November, farmers would move their CAVOLI from open fields to more sheltered areas and for the next four months countless heads were traded and sold at local markets and exported to northern Europe.

Farms in the Piedmont were usually quite small: families tilled their plots of land with a zealous independence characteristic of this Region's agriculture and which has helped protect it from the anonymity of so many fresh foods today. The growth of industry in the Canavese after World War II caused a decline in farming but new interest in quality, home-grown produce has led to a rebirth of Montaldo Dora's CAVOLO VERZA: its curly, cup-like leaves are well-suited to being stuffed, as for the local dish PESS-COJ (p. 36), their textured surface to being dipped into BAGNA CAODA (p. 20-33) as they "hold"

"Through the Fields", 1890.

Gesso sculpture by Davide Calandra (1856-1915); the GIPSOTECA, Museum of Plaster Casts in Savigliano (Cuneo) houses over 140 works by this Turin-born sculptor who, in addition to official public commissions, found inspiration in humble, realistic subjects, such as this one.

Typical
Rural
Architecture
of the
Canavese
Area

the sauce thanks to its cuplike leaves and their bumpy
texture and it is essential for a few traditional soups. This cabbage is
now even celebrated with its own country fair in late November but no
similar fate, as yet, has been reserved for its former consort whose position
was taken over by a tuber from the New World: the potato.

Grain is fundamental for the
following soups: three of them use
bread, recalling the origins of the
words soup & ZUPPA, the other uses
corn & wheat flour. Cabbage soup is
familiar to many people & turnip
soup probably imaginable but cheese

soup may seem a bit strange. For
those living in remote alpine valleys,
however, it was a delicious way of
eating the TOMA cheese produced in
many of the Piedmont's mountainous
areas: it can almost be thought of as
a sort of liquidy cheese sandwich,

very warm, filling, satisfying.
If TOMA cheese is not available,
FONTINA may be used. Homemade
broth is always recommended but, if
necessary, bouillon cubes may used:
they should be of the best quality
possible & not too salty.

92

Zuppa Canavese ～ 4 servings ～

3 ½ oz. PANCETTA (unsmoked ham), cut into thin strips
3 ½ oz. LARD, minced
2-4 cloves GARLIC, minced
2 LB. TURNIPS, peeled & sliced (or thinly sliced CABBAGE)
1 ½ QT. BEEF BROTH, boiling 8 slices crusty BREAD, toasted or sautéed in butter
grated PARMESAN CHEESE

1) Put the PANCETTA, LARD & GARLIC in a pot & lightly sauté over low heat.

2) Add the TURNIPS & cook 7-8 minutes. Add the BROTH & cook gently about ½ hour.

3) Preheat oven to hot (400-425°). Put 2-3 BREAD slices in an ovenproof casserole, cover them with 2 cups of the TURNIP-BROTH mixture & sprinkle with CHEESE. Repeat the layers 'til all the ingredients have been used, finishing with a topping of CHEESE. Bake about 20 minutes, 'til golden & crusty. Serve immediately.

Zuppa Barbetta traditional Waldenses soup ～ 4 servings ～

12 oz. crusty, stale BREAD, sliced
8 oz. TOMA or FONTINA CHEESE, sliced
grated PARMESAN CHEESE
1 QT. very hot BEEF or CHICKEN BROTH

Preheat oven to 350°. Arrange 2-3 BREAD slices in an ovenproof casserole & cover them with some of the sliced, then the grated, CHEESE. Repeat, forming 2-3 layers & add the BROTH. Bake about 20 minutes & serve.
VARIATIONS: GRISSINI (bread sticks), broken into medium-sized pieces, may be used instead of BREAD. Some people sprinkle a bit of CINNAMON over the CHEESE.

Zuppa Grassa from the Valle Susa ～ 4 servings ～

5 oz. very hard RYE BREAD
2 oz. BUTTER
5 oz. TOMA CHEESE
½ QT. BEEF BROTH
½ QT. WATER
1 small ONION, minced
grated NUTMEG
4 JUNIPER BERRIES, crushed

1) Pound the BREAD with a mortar & pestle 'til powdery & put in a pot with half the BUTTER & all the TOMA, both cut into bits. Add the BROTH & WATER & cook over low heat about ½ hour, stirring very often.

2) Put the remaining BUTTER, ONION, NUTMEG, BERRIES & a dash of PEPPER in a pan & cook 'til the ONION is wilted. Add this "sauce" to the BREAD-CHEESE mixture, stir well & serve immediately.

Puccia ～ 4 servings ～

1 LB. SAVOY CABBAGE, thinly sliced
1 LB. PORK LOIN, cut into small pieces
{**optional** 1 small ONION, CARROT & CELERY stalk, sliced}
1 QT. WATER, lightly salted
7 oz. CORN FLOUR
2 oz. WHITE FLOUR
2-4 TB. BUTTER, cut into bits
2-4 TB. grated PARMESAN CHEESE

1) Put the CABBAGE & PORK in a heavy pot with optional VEGETABLES & a glass of hot WATER, add a bit of SALT & cook, covered, over high heat 1-2 minutes, then over low-medium heat 20-30 minutes.

2) Bring the salted WATER to a boil & add the FLOUR, poured in a continuous flow, stirring constantly to prevent lumps from forming. Cook, stirring, 20-25 minutes, 'til smooth & creamy.

3) Add the CABBAGE-PORK mixture to the FLOUR & cook over moderate heat, stirring constantly for 20-25 minutes. If the consistency seems too thick, add a bit of boiling water. When done, add the BUTTER & CHEESE & serve immediately.

LEFTOVERS may be eaten in the following way: when cool, cut the PUCCIA into slices & fry them in very hot oil 'til a thin crust forms.

Bovines & Meat   Bovini e Carne

Few animals have given humanity, both materially and spiritually, as much as the bovine, or Bos taurus, L. Since time immemorial its milk, the cheese and butter made from it, and its meat have provided nourishment and as the primordial work animal, for thousands of years it pulled plows, carts and wagons all over the world, and still does in some places. Horses began to be harnessed in the Middle Ages but they served mostly for military purposes and oxen remained essential for producing the grains, legumes and vegetables that made the birth of cities possible and, in the Mediterranean world, continued to be so even after motorized machines were introduced in the 1800's: used in some parts of Italy 'til the 1950's, they have been replaced by tractors and reapers. In addition to their physical force, cattle's hides have long served for a variety of useful and luxurious leather goods, both a significant source of revenue and a showcase for masterful craftsmanship. Equally, if not more, important, though of a humbler nature, is the fertilizer these animals' manure provides that, until the 20th century's chemical imitations, was the best means of enriching the soil's fertility, thus increasing the supply of food. The benefits of the natural method are still recognized.

Bovines' exact origins are obscure: prevailing theories hold that today's varieties all derive from one primitive species or from several extinct ones. Cenozoic fossils have been found in China, India, North Africa and Europe and bovines continued to inhabit forests, tundra and steppe from Siberia and northern Europe to the Mediterranean into the 1600's, as seen in the, albeit limited, numbers of the great shaggy long-horned wild ox aurochs, or urus, that were roaming parts of Poland and Lithuania until then; it is now declared to be extinct. Their uncertain genesis has made it difficult to classify bovines but their well-developed frontal bone structure, coloring, four-part stomach and lack of upper incisor teeth were all proposed for doing so. However, it is their horns —long, short or absent- that best distinguish them: the size, position, angle and curve of these keratinous projections offer a myriad of variations that are now used for identifying different breeds of cattle.

Bronze Votive Statue late 2nd-early 3rd cent. Called APIS by the Egyptians, SERAPIS by the Greeks & Romans, this young bull was made in Industria (today, Monteu da Po, Monferrato), a Roman settlement famous for melting & molding metal. Museum of Antiquity, Turin

94

Votive Painting, oil on canvas, showing two successive moments of an accident. Shrine of St. Pancrazio, Vaglio Serra (Asti)

P.G.R. EMILIO PAVESE -VINCHIO-1912

These large, normally placid four-footed creatures have been an object of reverence since the remote past, as seen in Paleolithic cave paintings in France and Spain showing bulls and bison, presumed to have been done as part of sacred rituals performed before hunting expeditions. Domestication began around 6,000 B.C. in India and Egypt and about 3,500 B.C. in Europe and the Mediterranean area but taming this animal did not lessen its symbolic significance. For the Hittites in Asia Minor (c.2,000-700 B.C.) bulls were gods of storms, wind, lightning and thunder, Egyptians worshipped the sacred bull Apis and to this day, cows are holy for Hindus. Numerous ancient peoples expressed devotion by presenting burnt offerings of calves and heifers while the bull, symbol of strength, fertility and virility was the principal cult animal in the Mediterranean world and the protagonist of several Greek and Roman myths in which women were overcome with passion and lust for this powerful animal, the most famous being the beautiful young Phoenician princess, Europa: to seduce her, Zeus disguised himself as a friendly, alluring white bull and after she playfully climbed on his back, abducted her to Crete where she gave birth to Minos, who became king of that island. To affirm his throne, Minos was to sacrific a bull that the sea god Poseidon sent him but this beast was so magnificent, he kept it for his royal herd. To punish him, Poseidon made Minos' wife fall in love with this bull and their union gave birth to the Minotaur with a man's body

Rampant Bull, symbol of the city of Turin. Modified over the centuries, this example is from the 1400's

95

and a bull's head who lived unseen in the great palace of the labyrinth built especially for him by Daedalus. For the ancient Romans, bovines had an importance that went beyond religion: the plow used by Romulus, the legendary founder of Rome, to trace the form of this new city was pulled by two oxen, one male, one female, making this animal, in the words of the agrarian writer Columella (1ˢᵗ cent. A.D.), more glorious than any other, so revered that killing one was as serious a crime as killing a Roman citizen. For Christians, the ox symbolizes Christ's sacrifice and represents those who patiently and silently work for others and the ox in nativity scenes and St. Luke's winged bull are familiar subjects in Western art.

Ox,
detail from
"The Adoration",
predella of altarpiece
"Madonna & Saints" (c.1500)
by Defendente Ferrari,
from Chivasso,
active 1497-1531.
Sacra di San Michele,
Valle Susa (Turin)

In practical terms, for centuries bovines in Italy served mainly for work. Slaughtered only when they could no longer bear burdens or pull carts, their potential in the kitchen was ignored: the ancient Romans made cheese from goat's and sheep's milk, found butter distasteful, for meat, ate pork, lamb and goat. In short, they did not consider cattle a source of food and to this day, Italians eat less red meat than most other Europeans. Throughout the Middle Ages cow's milk was thought difficult to digest and it was only with the Renaissance that cheese made from it began to be appreciated, a food that, because associated with poor peasants and uncouth shepherds, had been disdained by the rich and noble who, instead, indulged in huge quantities of game. Hunting, in fact, was reserved almost exclusively for their entertainment and benefit, the most desirable prey being winged animals: according to the medieval vision of the cosmos, since they frequented the sky, closest to heaven, they were the most prized edible creatures. Although the early Church considered this activity pagan and uncivilized, the elite world of lords and courtiers ignored this Latin aversion and men and women alike willingly adopted the Germanic concept that identified the hunt with freedom and chivalry. This pastime, however, was to be thwarted by agricultural progress.

With the deforestation that was part of the rebirth of agriculture in the 12ᵗʰ century, the habitat of wild animals diminished in size as did the number of beasts

Peasant Plowing, from a late 12ᵗʰ cent. northern Italian DIGESTUM, a manuscript on legal questions. Library of Duomo, Ivrea

living there. Similarly, the open grazing lands that had sustained sheep and goats began to be cultivated and, like the woods, were transformed into fields of grain. Hay, especially alfalfa and clover introduced in the 1300's, became the main fodder, food more suited to bovines than game which stimulated cattle raising and even changes in warfare contributed to this. Before gunpowder arrived in Europe in the 1300's, cities and towns had to maintain sizable pastures for military horses —a particularly onerous obligation for the Piedmont due to its geographic vulnerability- but cannons made cavalry troops less necessary and cows took over this land. A reminder of this tradition is the place name PIAZZA D'ARME, or armament square, located on the periphery of commmunities throughout this Region, now occupied by stores, offices and private dwellings. The growing importance of cattle during the Middle Ages is seen in the numerous Piedmontese statutes issued regarding grazing rights and penalties for killing or harming bovines and by the 1500's they had become a significant source of income, sold and traded for their meat, milk and for work and their manure was a boon for farmers. Municipal funds were used to protect their health and local veterinarians began studying the epidemics that periodically devastated these animals.

The increase in bovines led to the practice of TRANSUMANZA, or transumance, from the Latin words trans, meaning over, across and humus, meaning earth, soil: the seasonal movement of livestock between lowlands and valleys in the winter and high alpine meadows in the summer with spring and fall intervals on the intermediary hillsides exploited the best, most nutricious forage each level offers. Still done today, starting in June, cows dine on the precocious lowest grasses; when these are consumed their "movable feast" gradually takes them up to 2,300 meters and by September the early crop, now regrown, is eaten as the animals descend. The Piedmont's landscape, with its extremely sweet and fragrant grasses in part responsible for some of Italy's best cheeses, is very well-suited to this migration. Today TRANSUMANZA is aided by trucks and most of us are hardly aware of it, but for centuries it was an important part of rural life. The day the cows left for the mountains people donned traditional clothes for special occasions, church bells tolled and an aura of festivity reigned.

19th cent. Festive Dress of the Valley of the Torrente Stura di Demonte which separates the Marittime & Cozie Alps. Museum of the City of Cuneo

97

Three of Italy's most prized breeds of cattle live in the Piedmont: the PIEMONTESE, VALDOSTANA and BRUNO-ALPINA, 'tho only the first is unique to this Region. Scientists believe it originated some 25,000 years ago when the Eurasian zebu, native to Asia and Africa, mated with the aurochs that inhabited the Piedmont. Physically striking, their hide is light gray to white (bulls are slightly darker), their large eyes are described as "expressive", "lively", their long tails end with thick fluffy tassels. Once valued as an outstanding work animal, particularly sought after for rice fields, this splendid beast, famous for its shapely rump, no longer touches a yoke. It is raised with great care and eats only quality corn, barley, wheat germ, hay and a few select vegetable products. While its milk is delicious, it is most appreciated for its tasty, lean meat, low in cholesterol, and better butcher shops in northern Italy often prominently display the word PIEMONTESE.

There are two main VALDOSTANA types: one has red spots, the other has black and both are essentially milk producers but like the PIEMONTESE, are also known for their veal. Today, these calves feed almost exclusively on whole milk, prevented from eating even hay until the end of their growth when cereal and chestnut flour, cooked potatoes and eggs may be added to their diet. The meat of the SANATO, as a milk-fed calf is called in the Piedmont, is light pink, barely marbled with fat, very tender, easily digested, rich in iron and usually rather expensive. Not surprisingly, Italian recipes for veal are favored by cooks and diners everywhere. The Swiss BRUNO-ALPINO, prized for its triple aptitude milk-meat-work, has been living on this side of the Alps so long it is regarded as almost indigenous here. Known for its calm temperment and remarkable resistence, it readily adapts to a variety of environmental and climatic conditions as proven by its successful migration to Eastern Europe, the Middle East, North Africa and the mid-west United States. It seems rather a paradox, given that these animals are raised to be butchered, that the perfection of certain breeds for this purpose means they are no longer threatened with extinction: after farming began to be mechanized in the 1800's,

Bronze Memorial Plaque for Ottavio Ottavi by Leonardo Bistolfi (1859-1933) on facade of Plaster Cast Museum of Bistolfi's work in their native city, Casale Monferrato.

The Ottavi brothers were leading figures in Italian agriculture 100 years ago. Their publishing company, BIBLIOTECA AGRARIA OTTAVI, devoted to all aspects of farming, produced scores of manuals on raising fruit, vegetables, livestock & grain, wine making (including the art of doing so in lean years), spring frosts, weather prediction, women & agriculture, fertilizers etc.

they became less necesary for plowing and risked becoming an endangered species. But, to-wards the end of the century, systematic attempts to improve the PIEMONTESE has meant that, ironically, their culinary excellence has preserved them.

However one may feel about digesting such delicacies as ox and veal brains, lungs, testicles, palate, ears, eyes and stomach, one cannot but admire the creativity of past cooks and their publics' lack of squeamishness. A taste for innards developed in the 1400's and they were used for making elaborate, extremely refined dishes; the animal's entire head was once a prized repast and Italian cookbooks of the 17th and 18th centuries offer numerous ways of preparing and presenting it, along with sweetbreads, cartilage, tongue, feet and tail and the more prosaic cuts eaten today. The quantity of these recipes indicates that, for those who afford it, beef had become quite present in Italian, and especially Piedmontese, cuisine and the fact that virtually nothing was wasted, nothing thrown away, merits the respect of the ecologically-minded even if not tempted by the menu. Entrails were common food in many places in the past and while prosperity has replaced them with other things, the Piedmont has not completely eliminated them: they are important for three of this Region's most famous dishes –FRITTO MISTO (mixed fry), BOLLITO MISTO (boiled meat) and LA FINANZIERA- which also include familiar cuts like filet, cutlet and liver, though due to such problems as "mad cow" disease, certain ingredients are no longer available. Another classic creation is beef braised in red wine, BRASATO AL BAROLO, distinguished by the union of this Region's superior cattle and red wine. It is interesting to read that ox meat was judged the best for both BRASATO and BOLLITO MISTO, preferably that of an animal that after five or six years of work, enjoyed at least six months of rest and an enriched diet.

1 round
2 rump
3 noisette, best cut of leg
4 outside cut
5 cut of leg
6 rump
7 cut of rump
8 loin, best for roasting
9 cut of loin
10 ribs
11 cut of ribs
12 neck
13 head
14 brains
15 cut of neck
16 gristle
17 hamstring
18 shoulder, cut in two
19 cutlet
20 round roast, larded
21 kidney, cut from loin
22 sweetbreads, larded with black truffles
23 fricandeau
24 loin filet, larded
25 slice of loin, for roasting
26 slice of leg, flattened & larded
27 snout, tongue

"Cuts of Veal & Other Quadrupeds" from "Trattato di Cucina, Pasticceria moderna, credenza e relativa confetturería" written & illustrated by Giovanni Vialardi (1804-1872), printed in Turin, 1854. Head chef for Italy's royal family in the 1800's, his book aimed to teach middle class dilettantes to make tasty dishes for formal meals. His precise measurements for ingredients are in the decimal metric system introduced in 1845. Royal Library, Turin. Every region in Italy has different names for certain cuts of beef. Charts in the "Enciclopedia Agraria Italiana" (Italian Agrarian Encyclopedia) show Turin having 25 cuts; Florence, 22; Palermo, 19; Genoa, Rome & Milan, 18; Naples & Venice, 17.

Mixed Boiled Meat — Bollito Misto

In the Piedmont, the rather insipid name BOLLITO MISTO, literally "boiled mixed", is totally deceiving. Often called GRAN BOLLITO MISTO, it truly is very grand in both contents and presentation and even has an aura of numerological mystique for traditinally it consisted of seven cuts of beef, seven "garnishes", seven boiled vegetables and at least three sauces, though today fewer ingredients are used. This magnificent combination, now rarely made at home, is the protagonist of one of gastronomy's most scenographic offerings: restaurants serve GRAN BOLLITO MISTO from a heated cart, diners watching and foretasting as the waiter skillfully and gracefully slices and prepares the steaming pieces they have chosen. At home, the meat and vegetables are arranged on a platter and cut at the table.

The art of carving meat, once as important as eating it, was imbued with cultural as well as functional significance, a vestige of its role in ancient religious sacrificial rituals. During the Middle Ages, and especially the Renaissance, this art was raised to new levels of perfection and the professional carver, or SCALCO, was a necessary figure in noble and wealthy households. Removing the maximum of an animal's edible parts with expertise and elegance, learned through training and experience, and knowing how to distribute them —a person's place in society determined the size, tenderness and quality of the pieces served- were performed in an atmosphere of respectful silence and numerous books were written on this subject. By the 1700's carving was no longer left exclusively to the SCALCO but, rather, was considered a skill indispensible for a gentleman. Undeniably, well-sliced meat is more attractive and, somehow, even seems more tasty.

BOLLITO MISTO is a festive dish, best made for at least 20 people, which allows for a rich and stunning array of ingredients: the contrast of the pink-red-brown meat with the round slices of sausage and the orange, green and white vegetables, their diverse shapes and textures, the sparkle of the coarse salt grains sprinkled just before serving, exemplify the proverbial phrase, "feast for the eyes". It is hardly worth making for less than ten people; leftovers, like the broth, are delicious and are used for filling AGNOLOTTI and certain vegetables. Eaten in many places in the Piedmont, this dish is especially honored in the town of Carrù

(Cuneo) where, since 1910, on the second Thursday before Christmas, the FIERA DEL BUE GRASSO, or Fat Ox Fair is held. Prizes are awarded for the most splendid examples of this animal, traditional music is performed and GRAN BOLLITO is served in the main square from morning 'til late evening and some restaurants also offer it. This dish's excellence is due only in part to the talent of local cooks, for it is the extraordinary quality of the RAZZA PIEMONTESE cattle that makes it unique. Obviously, this meat is not easily available outside this area but BOLLITO merits being made all the same.

traditional ingredients

BEEF: brisket, lean & fatty chops, haunch, rump, round, shoulder	GARNISHES: ox tail; veal head, tongue & foot; stewing hen or capon; COTECHINO sausage; meat loaf	VEGETABLES: cabbage, carrots, fennel, onions, potatoes, turnips, zucchini	SAUCES: Red (tomato); Green (parsley); others based on fruit, nuts, sweet-sour combinations (p. 102)

~ 10 servings ~

3-4 CARROTS, coarsely chopped
2 stalks CELERY, coarsely chopped
3 ONIONS, coarsely chopped
4 LB. BEEF (choose from list above)
2 LB. VEAL BRISKET
1 stewing HEN or CAPON
{**optional** 1 LB. VEAL HEAD without BRAINS }
1 LB. VEAL TONGUE
1 ½ LB. COTECHINO sausage

1) Put the VEGETABLES, BEEF & some SALT & PEPPER in a large pot with enough water to cover the MEAT. If BEEF is put in boiling water it will be more tasty but the BROTH will be less flavorful, if put in cold water, it will be less tasty but the BROTH will be more flavorful. Cover & simmer 1 hour. Add the VEAL & POULTRY & simmer 2 hours. This BROTH will be used.

2) In another pot, boil salted water & simmer the optional VEAL HEAD ½ hour, add the TONGUE & simmer 2 hours. This broth is discarded.

3) Soak the SAUSAGE in cold water 1 hour. Drain, pierce in a few places with a toothpick & put in a pot with cold water. Slowly bring to a boil over low heat & simmer 3 hours: the skin should not break. This broth is discarded.

The various lengths of cooking time should be considered when preparing this dish as the meats should be ready at the same time but if the BEEF-VEAL POULTRY wait in the BROTH a bit, this does no harm. The MEATS are sliced at the table, sprinkled lightly with coarse SALT, moistened with boiling BROTH & served with the VEGETABLES. The SAUCES are passed separately: interesting as they are, some people prefer the BOLLITO without them.

Two Views of Tuscan Farm Cart
from "Calendario Georgico" of the Royal Agrarian Society of Turin, 1827. A description of the cart's virtues –strong, light, stable- & precise construction is followed by the suggestion that it be adopted in the Piedmont. For the scholars who compiled this manual-like booklet, agriculture was the basis of a nation's prosperity: they aimed to educate farmers about cultivation techniques, enriching the soil & their crops, the health of livestock & included the Piedmont's principal fairs for the year: in Jan., 6; Feb., 10; Mar., 23; Ap., 40; May, 65; June, 31; July, 36; Aug., 91; Sept., 90; Oct.,73; Nov.,66; Dec., 0. The "Calendario" was printed by Giuseppe Pomba: this Turin publisher was a leading figure in 19th cent. efforts to make scientific information available to a general public. One of numerous enlightened reformers, he founded the "Nuova Enciclopedia Popolare" (new popular encyclopedia).

Historical Archive of the City of Turin

Sauces for Bollito Misto

BOLLITO MISTO is always served with at least one sauce and usually there are a few to choose from. These sauces embody some of the most salient characteristics of Piedmont cuisine: they are decisive, rich in flavor, "SAPORITE", or savory, not in the sense of piquant but, rather, in their having a distinctive, very particular taste and exemplify the fact that food in this Region is never insipid. They also present the interesting combinations of sweet and sour, or AGRODOLCE, the use of vinegar, mustard, honey etc. that are vestiges of Renaissance court cooking. In addition to eating with boiled meat, these SALSE are delicious with cooked vegetables. The ingredients suffice for 10 servings.

Green Sauce Salsa Verde

8 TB. fresh minced PARSLEY
1 clove GARLIC, minced
2-3 SALTED ANCHOVIES, rinsed & boned
2 ½ oz. BREAD, without crust
(Recipes in historic cookbooks show that in the past, bread was often used to thicken sauces)
½ cup WINE VINEGAR
1/2 – ¾ cup OLIVE OIL

Mix the PARSLEY, GARLIC & ANCHOVIES in a bowl. Soak the BREAD in the VINEGAR a few minutes, squeeze to remove moisture & stir into PARSLEY mixture. Gradually stir in the OIL: the sauce should be quite liquidy. Season to taste with SALT & PEPPER.

Red Sauce Salsa Rossa

1 ¼ lb. ripe TOMATOES,
1 CARROT, 2-3 medium ONIONS, chopped
2-3 cloves GARLIC, minced
tiny piece HOT RED PEPPER
1 TB. RED WINE VINEGAR
1-2 TB. SUGAR, OLIVE OIL

Put the ingredients in a pot with 1-2 spoonfuls of OLIVE OIL & a pinch of SALT. Cook slowly for 3-4 hours. Strain & thin with a bit of OLIVE OIL & taste for SALT.

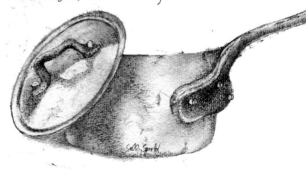

Honey Sauce Salsa delle Api

24 WALNUTS, shelled
4-5 TB. BROTH or WATER
2 TB. strong MUSTARD
12–16 oz. fluid HONEY

Blanch the NUTS in boiling water about 30 seconds, drain & remove their thin skin. Pound them to a powder with a mortar & pestle & put in a bowl. Stir in the BROTH or WATER & the MUSTARD & mix well. Add the HONEY & stir 'til smooth & creamy.

Poorman's Sauce Salsa del Pover'uomo

7 EGGS
3 TB. FLOUR
1-2 TB. SALT
3 oz. BUTTER
2-3 cloves GARLIC, minced
4 TB. RED WINE VINEGAR

Break the EGGS into a bowl & with a fork, gently beat in the FLOUR & SALT. Heat the BUTTER & GARLIC in a pan: when the BUTTER begins to foam, stir the VINEGAR into the EGGS & immediately add them to the GARLIC. Cook over low heat, stirring with a wooden spoon 'til the mixture becomes creamy.

102

La Finanziera

LA FINANZIERA is one of the Piedmont's most famous, almost legendary, dishes. Its name, literally "frockcoat", is thought to derive from the fact that it was once a favorite lunch of Turin's bankers, businessmen and parliament members who, in the 1800's often wore this long, double-breasted full-skirted overcoat. However, in his dictionary of Piedmont gastronomy, Sandro Doglio suggested that FINANZIERA was a tax that farmers had to pay when they brought their poultry to sell in Turin's markets and took the form of the fowls' giblets, crests and wattles which they gave to the FINANZIERI, the guards controlling entry into the city, for whom this dish was named. It is interesting that in French cooking "a là financière" refers to a garnish consisting of these very ingredients. It is not as popular as it once was, perhaps because coxcombs and wattles have lost some of their culinary appeal —some recipes also call for bull's testicles- nor are sweetbreads a big favorite, but an abbreviated version more in line with today's tastes can be made. In any case, the mere description of how to render the rooster's crest and fleshy chin edible is sufficiently intimidating to make one relieved that they are not easy to find. Without them LA FINANZIERA lacks some of its character, but the other ingredients —chicken livers, veal, beef- cut in small pieces, lightly floured and cooked in butter are made more exotic by the addition of mushrooms, vinegar and dry Marsala.

~ 4 servings ~

5 oz. ROOSTER CREST & WATTLE
3 oz. each of VEAL SWEET-
    BREADS, SPINE MARROW &
    RUMP
3 oz. BEEF FILET
3 oz. CHICKEN LIVER
1½ oz. BUTTER
    FLOUR
2 oz. MUSHROOMS conserved
    in VINEGAR, chopped
1 TB. each WINE VINEGAR &
    DRY MARSALA

1) Put the CREST & WATTLE in a pot, add water to cover & a pinch of SALT. Heat & as soon as the water gets warm, using one's hands, rub the CREST & WATTLE to see if their skin comes off. If no, leave over heat a bit longer, if yes, drain & put on a tea towel & sprinkle with SALT. With the towel, rub off any remaining skin, pierce them with a needle (to prevent bursting) & soak in salted water to cover 4 hours, changing the water a few times. They should become white.

2) Put the SWEETBREADS in a pot, cover with water & boil 5 minutes. Cool under running water, drain, remove their skin & thinly slice.

3) Cut the MEAT, MARROW, SWEETBREADS & LIVER in nut-sized pieces & dust them with FLOUR. Melt the BUTTER in a large pan & add the FILET, RUMP & a bit of SALT & lightly brown. Add the CREST, WATTLE, MARROW & then the SWEETBREADS & LIVER. When they are half-cooked, add the MUSH-ROOMS. Cook over low heat, stirring occasionally to prevent sticking. When the contents are almost done, add the VINEGAR & MARSALA. Taste & if it seems too strong, add a pinch of SUGAR. Serve very hot in vol-au-vents or with plain white rice.

Fritto Misto

Many places in Italy have their own typical FRITTO MISTO, "fried-mixed", which may consist of meat, seafood or vegetables but none offer as rich an example of this dish as the Piedmont where it is a model for the concept of the maximum. In the past, its basic ingredients numbered around twenty; today they are less but optional ones are still unlimited and present a contrast of tastes ranging from strong to delicate, bitter to sweet, piquant to mild. The traditional FRICIA PIEMONTESE includes veal, pork, lamb and poultry –innards as well as meat-, sausage, vegetables, rice and potato croquettes, fruit, diamond-shaped pieces of sweet semolina pudding and this Region's wonderful soft almond macaroons, AMARETTI. Thus, it is a one-course meal. Its laborious preparation requires much handwork (cleaning, soaking, boiling, draining, peeling, chopping...), numerous frying pans and highly organized kitchen choreography: all the components must be served at the same time and since they must be eaten hot, as soon as they are fried, their different lengths of cooking time must be well understood and calculated. The Piedmont's FRITTO batter is richer than in most other places: the ingredients, cut into small pieces, are dipped first in flour, then in beaten egg and finally, in bread crumbs, then quickly fried in oil, a cooking method Italians are masters at.

This dish, eaten for special occasions and holidays, is now rarely made at home, mostly enjoyed in restaurants where it is normally ordered in advance and ceremoniously served from large platters laden with the various ingredients artistically arranged. Impressive in both content and execution, FRICIA might not appeal to everyone but it unquestionably merits respect and admiration; historic cookbooks make clear that in the past almost nothing was discarded and this dish is a stunning example of how to create something quite grand from bits and pieces. Many of us are not tempted by tidbits of veal brains, heart, kidneys, lungs, spinal marrow, sweetbreads or testicles, rooster crests and wattles, pigs' feet etc. but if they do not excite the stomach, they stimulate the imagination. I admit they do not arouse my appetite and rather regret that I can only appreciate them mentally, feeling as if I have lost something I never had, that is, the

from
butcher
stalls ,
**Porta
Palazzo
Market**, Turin
A-Veal Brains
B-Pig's Foot
C-Sweetbreads
D-Lungs **E**-Kidneys

ability to savor those "throw-away" parts that were once a vital feature of people's diets. In any case, the possibility of trying them is limited for they are often difficult to find today. No two recipes for FRITTO MISTO are alike and, fortunately, it has something for everyone: lamb and veal cutlets, chicken, mushrooms, eggplants, zucchini —and their brilliant yellow flowers- carrots, artichoke hearts, apples, pears, cookies...

Artichokes, not traditional in the Piedmont, are an "import" from nearby Liguria

Ingredients depend on the season & on local products but AMARETTI & lozenges of SEMOLINA are almost always included, plus a selection from the following:

VEAL: brains, liver, spinal marrow, sweetbreads
PORK: chop, liver, sausage
LAMB: chop
CHICKEN: crest, wattle, croquette
VEGETABLES: eggplant, zucchini, artichoke hearts
FRUIT: apple, pear
CROQUETTES: rice, potato, chicken
BRAINS: soak in cold water 1 hour, then blanch in boiling salted water 3 minutes
SPINAL MARROW: soak in cold water 1 hour, put in a pot of cold water & when it comes to a boil, drain
SWEETBREADS: Soak in cold water a few hours, changing water a few times, then simmer 5 minutes in salted water & drain
FLOUR
BEATEN EGGS
BREAD CRUMBS
{**optional** grated NUTMEG}
OLIVE OIL
{**optional** VEGETABLE OIL}
MILK —for soaking the AMARETTI

When the ingredients have been cleaned etc., cut them into small pieces. Dip them in FLOUR, then in the bread crumbs: exceptions are the SAUSAGE, which goes directly into the boiling OIL without any batter & the AMARETTI, which are soaked briefly in MILK, then gently squeezed & dipped in BREAD CRUMBS. Fry the various ingredients in abundant boiling OIL; the VEGETABLES may be fried in VEGETABLE OIL & a bit of NUTMEG may be added to their BREAD CRUMBS. When something is being fried, never add new OIL for this lowers the temperature. The most difficult aspect of this dish is to have all of its contents ready at the same moment, considering their varying frying times. As soon as they are removed from the OIL, serve, sprinkling with a bit of SALT at the last minute.

Beef Braised in Red Wine — Brasato Al Barolo

Until the 20th century most of the beef eaten in Italy came from oxen, animals accustomed to wearing a yoke that had spent their lives pulling plows and wagons and butchered only when no longer fit for such work. Their meat was lean, their muscle fiber tough, best prepared by braising: this slow cooking in little liquid relaxes and tenderizes the muscles and facilitates their absorbing the aromas and flavors of the other ingredients. This meat, prized for its taste and texture, greatly due to years of physical labor, is no longer available, eliminated by the motorized machines that, starting in the late 1800's, did much to make farmers' lives easier: by the 1960's, tractors etc. had definitively replaced animals in Italian agriculture. Today, BRASATO is made from local beef cattle, the best being the PIEMONTESE whose notable natural qualities are reinforced by a singularly healthy diet that contains no industrially produced animal feed and consists only of hay, corn, bran, barley and a variety of legumes. While beef braised in red wine is not unique to the Piedmont, this Region's bovines and Barolo wine make this Italy's most celebrated version of this dish. In addition to the fragrance of the sauce, one is struck by its rich, warm brown color, almost luminescent, as it coats the sliced meat, its consistency both pleasingly firm and tender. When ox meat was used for BRASATO, it was usually marinated, as in the recipe below.

Marinated Version ~ 4 servings ~

2 LB. piece of BEEF, rump or round
2 CARROTS, 2 ONIONS, 2 CELERY
stalks, all coarsely chopped
Tied in cotton gauze: 1 sprig
ROSEMARY, 2 LAUREL leaves,
small piece of CINNAMON,
3 CLOVES, 3 PEPPER GRAINS,
1 clove GARLIC, pinch of grated
NUTMEG, 3 JUNIPER BERRIES,
3 SAGE leaves
1 bottle BAROLO WINE
2 oz. BUTTER
1/3 cup COGNAC or BRANDY

1) Put the MEAT, VEGETA-
BLES, SEASONINGS & WINE in a ceramic
casserole, cover & let marinate from 6–48
hours in a cool place, but not in refrigerator.
Stir occasionally.

2) Remove the MEAT; drain it, pre-
serving the MARINADE. Melt the
BUTTER in a heavy pot with a lid
& brown the MEAT in it, turning
to cook all over. Add the COGNAC:
flambé til the flame goes out.

3) Add the MARINADE & the
VEGETABLES. Cook, covered, very
slowly, for 2 hours. Remove the VEG-
ETABLES, purée them with the cooking
juices, add a dash of SALT & PEPPER &
pour over the MEAT. Cover & cook very
slowly for 1-2 hours.

4) Slice the MEAT –not too thinly-
& serve with the cooking juices. Mashed potatoes usually accompany this dish.

Juniper Berries growing wild on the slopes around
Sestriere (Turin)

Non-Marinated Version ~ 4 servings ~

2 LB. piece of BEEF, rump, round or loin

small piece of LARD, cut into strips

FLOUR

1 TB. fresh minced PARSLEY

3-4 SAGE leaves, minced

½ TB. ROSEMARY leaves, minced

1 clove GARLIC, minced

pinch of grated NUTMEG & CINNAMON

2 CLOVES

3 TB. OLIVE OIL

3 TB. BUTTER

1 small ONION, thinly sliced

1 CARROT, sliced

1 CELERY stalk, chopped

2 LAUREL leaves

a few PARSLEY sprigs

1 bottle BAROLO WINE

1) Lard the BEEF: the strips are easier to insert, always following the grain, if they are chilled. Dust the BEEF with FLOUR.

2) Put the HERBS, GARLIC & SPICES in a bowl with a dash of SALT & PEPPER & mix well.

3) Heat the OIL & BUTTER in a large heavy pot with a lid & lightly sauté the ONION. Put in the BEEF, sprinkle with the HERB-SPICE mixture & add the VEGETABLES, LAUREL leaves & PARSLEY. Lightly brown the MEAT all over, then remove it. Skim off any excess fat from the pot's contents & stir in a spoonful of FLOUR, mixing 'til well blended over low heat. Pour in a glass of WINE & cook 'til the liquid reduces a bit. Return the BEEF to the pot, turning it to coat with the HERBS & VEGETABLES. Add the remaining WINE.

4) Cover & cook very slowly for 3 -4 hours, stirring occasionally. When the MEAT is done –it should be very tender- remove the LAUREL leaves. Press the VEGETABLES & cooking juices through a strainer to make a dense sauce. Add SALT if necessary. Slice the BEEF & serve with the heated sauce. This dish is usually accompanied by mashed potatoes.

Brentatore by Gallo Gallina from "Costumi dei contorni di Torino" (traditions of the environs of Torino) published by Pietro Martinetti in Turin, 1834. In the Piedmont, the BRENTA was a liquid measure, usually 49.184 liters & the word also referred to a large basket for transporting wine that the BRENTATORE carried on his shoulders (p. 167). He was responsible for measuring the amount, & calculating the cost, of wine bought & sold & for delivering it to wine merchants' customers. A respected profession dating back at least to the 1500's, it was organized in a hierarchy of roles passed on from father to son with the majority of the BRENTATORI coming from the Valleys of Lanzo & Sesia. In the 1500's they were officially authorized to oversee & regulate this trade, a privilege that included civic & social obligations: in case of fire, they had to carry water in their BRENTA to extinguish it & they could not eat or drink with wine clients nor receive any money from them. The BRENTATORE was easily recognized by his blue smock & the wooden container & ladle he carried on a shoulder strap: the PONGONE held 1.369 liters. The closing of public wine markets in the 1800's led to their demise: there had been hundreds of them throughout the Piedmont (see p. 167). The BRENTA was gradually replaced by the decimal metric system, created in France in the 1790's, legalized in 1799 & made obligatory in 1837. It was approved by law in the Piedmont in 1845 & as Italy moved toward unification this system began to be adopted in other parts of the peninsula. Nonetheless, the many different units of measure that had been used for centuries –almost every city had its own- continued to prevail. They were based on intuitive, empirical, practical concepts such as the amount of liquid a container could hold & be carried by one person a long or short distance or the use of the arm or foot of an average adult male for establishing a standard of length. In the Middle Ages there was an attempt to use symbolic, "spiritual" measurements such as the BRACCIO TORINESE, or arm of Turin, based on the presumed signs of Christ's body on the Holy Shroud, kept in that city. The metric system was too abstract & mathematical for most people who preferred the visual, functional references they were familiar with which, especially in rural areas, continued to be used throughout the 1800's.

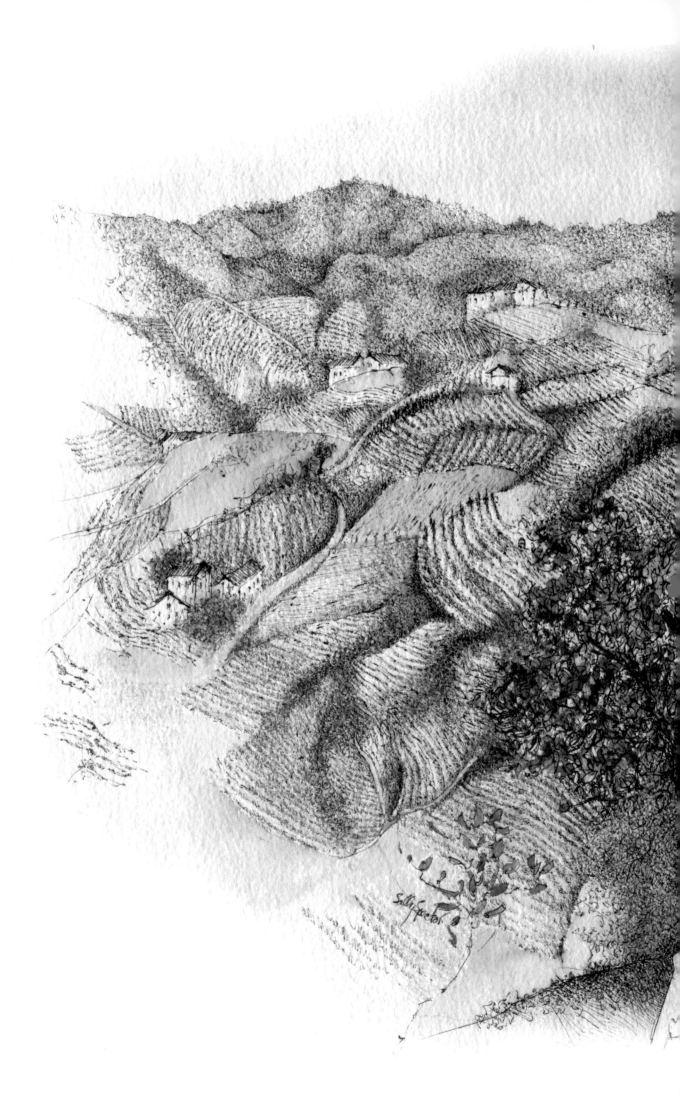

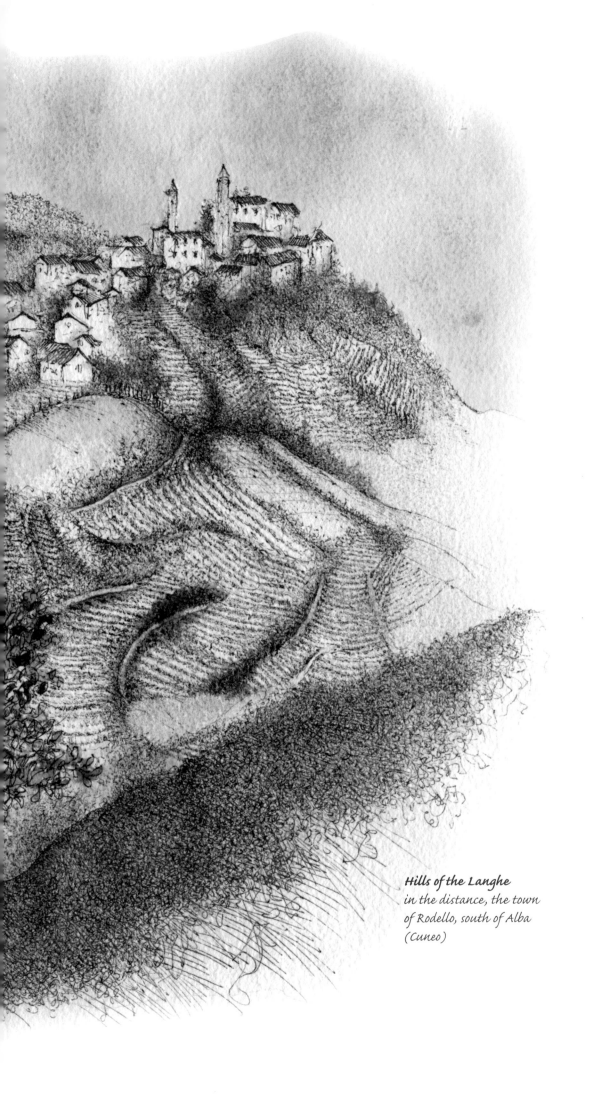

Hills of the Langhe
*in the distance, the town
of Rodello, south of Alba
(Cuneo)*

Truffles   Tartufi

The Latin word tuber, meaning hump, knob and tumor, which became tufera in vulgar Latin, is the presumed origin of the English word truffle and the Italian TARTUFO (the English word tube derives form the Latin tubus, meaning pipe). Truffle is the common name for several species of ascomycetous fungi of the genus Tuber –in Europe at least 30 have been identified- which reproduce by spores generated in a sac-like structure called ascocarp. Native to temperate regions, the truffle lives from 20 to 50 centimeters below ground and like all fungi, it does not produce flowers or seeds nor does it have roots, stems or leaves: it exists thanks to the symbiotic relationship it establishes with the roots of certain trees, mostly oaks and poplars but also lindens and willows. This intimate rapport, called mychorrhiza, is a complex and extremely efficient system of exchange of great benefit for both parties which provides them with essential nourishment that they are incapable of getting on their own. The truffle forms a sort of muff of varying density around the tips of the tree's roots and avails itself of the sugar accumulated there from photosynthesis. The truffle cells, functioning like root hairs, virtually increase the roots' surface area, enabling them to stretch further through the earth to better exploit the soil's minerals and facilitate water absorption.

Truffles are generally classified by their color –black or white- and provenance: acclaimed for their unique flavor, they are among the world's most expensive delicacies. The most famous black ones, Tuber malanosporum vittadini, come from the Piedmont, central Italy and the Perigord region in France. Their ebony surface is covered with tiny bumps, their dark flesh is marbled with white veins. But, far more prized and costly are the Piedmont's white truffles, Tuber magnatum Pico, officially classified and named in 1788 by the Piedmontese botanist Vittorio Pico. Actually more beige than white, they are also known as TARTUFI BIANCHI D'ALBA, after the city that hosts the most famous of the numerous truffle fairs held every year from September to December and come mostly from the Langhe Monferrato-Roero area. As proof that

Black Truffles woodcut from "I Discorsi" by Sienese physician Pier Andrea Mattioli (1500-1577). His interpretation of & comments on the writings of the ancient Greek scientist Pedanius Dioscorides which describes the therapeutic properties of plants was an essential reference for physicians before modern, scientific medicine was born. Edition printed in 1675, in Venice. Marciana Library, Venice

TARTVFFI

looks are not everything, thousands of dollars have been paid for exceptional examples of white truffles: usually said to resemble potatoes, their surface is quite smooth while their form is very irregular, with little knob-like protuberances that give them a gnarled look and if one did not know what they are, they would not evoke much interest. Their firm interior, from white to pink to yellow to gray, is crossed by white veins. These nondescript features are more than compensated for by their unmistakable odor and flavor. The best ones live with oaks, rarely in forests but, rather, with single, isolated trees. This tree prefers dense, compact soil and the moist, clayish terrain, rich in lime and silica, of the area around Alba offers the most favorable environment for its union with truffles: the oak's roots dig down deeply, resulting in TARTUFI that are not only harder to find, they are heavier, and often more fragrant, more regular in shape and darker than others. They can be more than 10 centimeters in diameter and weigh more than 500 grams but whatever their dimensions, they are a significant source of revenue for the hundreds of truffle hunters in the Piedmont, TRIFOLAI in Piedmontese, TARTUFAI in Italian.

The TRIFOLAO is a somewhat legendary figure who, in foggy, melancholy autumn weather hunts for truffles to show and sell at markets and fairs. He usually does this after dark, to keep his movements as secret as possible and is careful not to reveal where potential finds might be: an aura of mystery has thus developed around this taciturn personage. His only company is a specially trained dog, often a mixture of setter and hound but mongrels can be excellent; in central Italy, a sow is often used.

Truffle Hunter or TRIFOLAO, engraving from "I Tartufi", by Giambernardo Vigo, printed in Turin, 1776. Written in Latin, translated into Italian, this work in rhyme, tho not scientific, discusses where, how & when to find TARTUFI, how to use, cut & preserve them. Marciana Library, Venice.

Only those animals that show an exceptionally keen sense of smell are selected for this activity and "school" begins at about six months of age. At first they are given a tiny piece of black truffle –white are too expensive- to play with, like a ball, and then, to eat. What started as a game turns into instruction as the puppy learns to detect the penetrating smell of TARTUFI from a distance: a nugget of truffle is hidden in increasingly concealed places, from inside a shoe to a hole in the ground and its discovery is awarded with some tasty morsel, to prepare for the real hunt in the open. Once a tuber is located, the animal starts digging with its paws and snout and the TRIFOLAO takes over, using his hands or a small spade. Since a pig tends to gobble up the precious object before its master gets to it, dogs are usually preferred but some findings can be made without the help of either. Truffles close to the earth's surface can cause it to bulge or crack in ways that only a skilled TARTUFAO can recognize and thumping on this produces a distinctive sound and a whiff of their aroma. There is also a particular fly attracted by the truffle's odor so that a hovering swarm of this miniscule insect may sign its presence. Romantic as this activity might seem, it is actually very painstaking and its results are often disappointing: the TARTUFO is even more secretive and elusive than its hunter and rests tranquil and cosy in its den of roots.

Truffle Seller, colored engraving by Gallo Gallina from "Costumi dei contorni di Torino" (traditions of the environs of Turin) printed by Pietro Marinetti in Turin, 1834.

Historic Archive of the city of Turin

Truffles are extremely difficult, if not impossible, to cultivate. "Planting" them, TARTUFICOLTURA, involves sprinkling a mushy, pulpy mixture made from tiny pieces of mature TARTUFI diluted with water in a forest of specially pruned oak trees and then, waiting. If successful, it takes about ten years before a crop can be harvested but this method has not yielded satisfying results and thus the experienced TRIFOLAI and their seemingly primitive techniques remain indispensable. Thanks to modern research, however, the symbiotic phenomenon of mycorrhiza is now understood and applied to agriculture, where "sowing" these fungi can reduce certain plants' needs for chemical fertilizer, and to forestry, which uses tubers in reforestation programs in areas with poor, infertile soil. But, this knowledge is of recent date: for centuries, truffles were very puzzling and very, very hard to fathom.

Pliny the Elder clearly expressed this perplexity in the 1ˢᵗ century A.D. in his "Natural History"; he realized truffles had no roots but were nonetheless intimately connected with the soil that completely surrounded them and questioned if they were alive or not and if they underwent stages of development. He was certain they were not generated by seeds and wondered if they were a sign of sickness or perhaps were callouses of the very earth they seemed to be made of. Since they were mostly found in autumn, he imagined that the frequent rain and thunder during that season provoked their presence. His work is also the source for the much repeated reference to a Roman magistrate who damaged his front teeth while chewing a truffle that had a pebble or other hard oject in it which led to the belief that eating them was dangerous for one's dentures. Pliny was indifferent to their culinary qualities, as was the Greek physician Galen (2nd cent. A.D.) who thought that in addition to being difficult to digest, they caused melancholy and even apoplexy. Such ideas, however, had little influence on wealthy ancient Greeks and Romans for whom they were a delicacy; the oldest cookbook known to us, "De re coquinaria" (on cooking), by Apicio (1st. cent. A.D.), albeit an incomplete 4th century version of the original, includes among its nearly 500 recipes a few using these tubers. In addition to their gastronomic merits, it was believed they were aphrodisiac, that eating them strengthened virility. After the fall of the Roman Empire in 476, like many other luxury foods, truffles all but disappeared from the kitchen and their association with sexual performance was replaced by Galen's opinion. For example, the Arab philosopher and physician Ibn Sina, better known as Avicenna (980-1037), believed they were tasteless and provoked apoplexy and sadness and Europeans of his day linked them with the devil and evil spirits: their coming from damp, dark, underground places helped reinforce this negative connotation.

Terra Cotta Frieze, 15th cent. Casa Fontana, Alba (Cuneo)

Things were to change, however —perhaps influenced by the discovery of Apicio's book in the mid-1400's- and the virtues of truffles were once again appreciated, though these were almost exclusively black ones as the Piedmont was still quite estraneous to the rest of Italy. Those of Norcia are specifically referred to in one of the most famous cookbooks of all time, "De honesta voluptate et valetudine" (honest pleasure and good health), by Bartolomeo Sacchi, known as "il Platina" (1421-1481), printed in Latin in 1475 in Rome and in Italian in Venice in 1507. Due to their reputed aphrodisiac properties, he wrote, truffles were often served at the elegant banquets of refined gentlemen so as to better prepare themselves for the "pleasures of Venus"; a moralist as well as a cook, he added that if procreation were the purpose of such acts, eating them was justified, even praiseworthy, but if they were merely libidinous, eating them was detestable. A century later, the Roman physician and botanist Castore Durante (1523-1590), author of two very popular books – "Herbario novo" (new herbal) and "Il tesoro della sanità" (treasure of health)- repeated Pliny's likening of truffles to callouses but also emphasized their erotic qualities: rich people ate them, he wrote, to excite their sexual appetites and called black ones "male" and white ones "female". But, he considered them not very good, difficult to digest, a cause of melancholy and, as the Roman magistrate well knew, "enemies of the teeth". In "Trattato della natura de' cibi e del bere" (treatise on food and drink) printed in Venice in 1587, another medical doctor, Baldassarre Pisanelli from Bologna, wrote that these tubers not only increased carnal desire, but also sperm quantity. Even after 500 years these words are strikingly relevant: the idea that TARTUFI could benefit lovemakng may seem ingenuously amusing now but it is interesting to note that scientific research done at the University of Munich show they contain a volatile alcohol that smells like musk, a substance present in the male musk deer's abdomen, that is closely associated with the male sex hormone testosterone.

In contrast to the writers just mentioned, the author of the most important 16th century work on botany expressed no interest in truffles and sex and briefly mentions that they may be eaten raw or cooked. Pier Andrea Mattioli, after saving his earnings from practicing medicine, first in his native Siena, then in Rome, Trento and Gorizia and serving as Court Physician for the Hapsburg rulers Ferdinand I and his son, Maximillian II, dedicated himself to the natural sciences and wrote a commentary on the works of Pedanius Discurides (1st cent A.D) with the addition of all information pertaining to medical botany that had become available since antiquity. As revealed in "I Discorsi", first printed in Venice in 1544, he was, like Pliny, baffled by the true nature of

Two Couples from 15th cent. frescoes in the Great Hall of the Castle of Manta (Saluzzo), depicting the "Fountain of Youth", attributed to Giacomo Jacquerio & his circle. While elderly knights & ladies are undressing, about to get in the water, others who have already lost their wrinkles & gray hair are once agan feeling amorou also seen the clothea couple where the ma is ardently wooing hesitant woman.

*frescoes were reproduced in the "Medieval"
...built in Turin in 1884 under the
...ion of Alfredo D'Andrade
...-1915). From Lisbon,
...me to Italy to study
...dedicated himself
...toring monuments
...Piedmont & Valle
...a. The Castle of
...a belongs to
...ONDO PER
...BIENTE
...ANO*

truffles, wondering too if they were alive. For
Mattioli, they seemed to consist of the same material as the earth, as if a condensed, concentrated
form of it, born but not planted, perplexity also
expressed by a few 20th century scientists
who proposed that TARTUFI are neither
plants nor animals and a third category
should be created just for them.

While Mattioli was pondering over
phytographic questions, his contemporary
Bartolomeo Scappi, personal chef of a Cardi-
nal and of Pope Pius V, was preparing sumptuous meals for the Papal Court in Rome. His
book entitled simply "Opera" (work), published in Venice in 1570 and reprinted numerous times –considered by some the greatest cookbook ever written- includes several
dishes made with truffles such as a soup, a FRITTATA (Italian version of an omelette) and
a recipe for stewing them as well as the suggestion that they could be eaten raw with a bit
of salt and pepper. Although Scappi's position in the ecclesiastical world might have hindered any mention of truffles and sensuality, it is also possible that his silence on this subject
is evidence of the fact that TRIFOLI were beginning to be appreciated primarily for their
culinary qualities, regardless of any after effects. However, the sugar, exotic spices and the
sweet and sour and bitter orange sauces his recipes call for, the strong flavors characteristic
of Renaissance Court cuisine, would have competed with, and perhaps overpowered, the
truffles' distinctive taste which is also weakened by prolonged cooking. In the following decades such recipes appear with increasing frequency and truffles are used in stews, casseroles,
sauces and rice dishes accompanied by saffron, cinnamon, sugar, nutmeg, thyme, garlic,
prunes, liver, pork sausage and parmesan cheese.

Cooking, like many aspects of life, was affected by political and economic events. Italy's
predominance among Europe's cuisines was waning as France, especially under Louis XIV,
became the new model for the culinary arts. Thus it is not surprising that a cook from the
Piedmont, the most "French" part of Italy, but which had not yet produced any significant
such writings, was the anonymous author of one of the most important Italian cookbooks of
the 1700's, in which TARTUFI BIANCHI PIEMONTESI are specifically called for. In "Il
Cuoco piemontese perfezionato a Parigi" (piedmontese cook perfected in Paris), printed in

Cinnamon,
woodcut from "Herbario Novo"
by Castore Durante(1523-1590),
printed in Venice, 1617.
Marciana Library, Venice

Turin in 1766 and reprinted 22 times over the next hundred years, tribute is fully paid to the Tuber magnatum Pico, described as the best condiment available, but still combined with spices and mashed or chopped for sauces and stuffings or roasted for an hour on hot embers. In addition to their use in the kitchen, white truffles were one of the gifts given to eminent and powerful people as a sign of respect or in the hope of obtaining their favor, as did Pinerolo's Princes of Acaja in the late 1300's and the Dukes of Savoy often sent them to foreign rulers while sometimes, they were requested, as when the French King Louis XVIII (1755-1824) asked for "friendly" shipments of them.

How truffles were liberated from cinnamon and cloves and began to be enjoyed on their own is not totally clear but economic and social factors certainly played a part. The discovery of new trade routes and the flourishing commerce with the East Indies from the 16th to the 19th century meant that exotic spices, once reserved exclusively for the wealthy, became cheaper and more accessible; thus, they lost much of their allure as status symbols, plainer, more natural tastes turned fashionable and the TARTUFO was free to be savored alone. Credit for this is also due to Giovanni Vialardi, from Salussola, near Biella. He was head chef for Italy's royal family, serving under Carlo Alberto (1831-1849) and Vittorio Emanuele II (1849-1878), but is most remembered for his book, "Trattato di cucina pasticceria moderna credenza e relativa confetturia" printed in Turin in 1854, which, in spite of the regal environment he worked in, was meant to instruct dilettantes to prepare family dinners as simply as possible. The growth of a comfortable, literate middle class in northern Italy in the 1800's led to an ever increasing number of books on cooking, healthy eating, hygiene and home economics and Vialardi addressed himself to this new public: like the anonymous "perfected" Piedmontese before him, he also specifies white truffles for the recipes designated as "ALLA PIEMONTESE" which to this day indicates the presence of Tuber magnatum Pico. They were no longer stewed or transformed into a purée or sauce but, instead, added raw, thinly sliced, to a dish just before serving it, as they are normally eaten nowadays, and best savored.

Called the diamonds of the culinary world by the French gastronome Anthelme Brillat-Savarin (1755-1826), white truffles are associated with particular dishes. Some people claim they are best with fried or scrambled eggs but they are also sliced on TAJARIN (p. 81), rice and raw meat. They are now used to flavor some local cheeses but it is generally felt that their addition to a seemingly unlimited variety of dishes and prepared foods is more for snob appeal than the palate and truffles do not lend themselves to being preserved. The TARTUFO BIANCO needs no promotion but much of its current popularity is thanks to a restaurateur from Alba, Giacomo Morra, who, in the1950's revived the historic practice of giving an impressive specimen to a prominent person every year: Winston Churchill, Harry S. Truman, Charles De Gaulle, the Pope...were among such recipients and this homage resulted in excellent publicity. People who may never see, let alone eat, a Tuber magnatum Pico know of its existnce and today a sort of gastronomic tourism attracts thousands of visitors to the Langhe during the truffle season to buy, eat or just look at them. Their price puts them beyond most pocketbooks but older people remember when the TARTUFI were less famous, the hills had more trees for the tubers to live with –even children occasionally found them- and it was possible to eat them for a very special occasion.

Truffles should feel solid and a bit hard to the touch; their odor should suggest garlic and hay and those hinting of ammonia should be discarded. Surface dirt is best removed with a medium-stiff brush, damp sponge or soft cloth and bruise marks should be cut away. A specially designed instrument is recommended for slicing them. Not to be confused with them are TARTUFI eaten as sweets: little mounds of chocolate and vanilla ice cream and balls of pure chocolate, their vague resemblance to the underground fungus explains their name. More difficult to understand is why the word TARTUFO also refers to a person who pretends to be something he or she is not, a figure present in Italy's COMMEDIA DELL'ARTE from at least the early 1600's, which was probably the source for the French playwright Moliere's satirical comedy about a religious hypocrite, Le Tartuffe, written in the 1600's. If anything, truffles, both black and white, are much, much more than they seem.

Truffle Slicer

Cheese   Formaggio

According to Greek mythology, the shepherd Aristeus, son of the nymph Cirene and Apollo, protector of agriculture and grazing, introduced cheesemaking to humanity but it was likely discovered by chance, when it was noted that milk gone sour separated into solid curds and watery whey and thus goes back to the distant past. In the ancient Mediterranean world cheese was made almost exclusively from sheep's and goat's milk, that of donkeys was popular among Arabs and the "father of medicine", the Greek physician Hippocrates (460-370 B.C.) saw horse's milk used when he went to gather medicinal herbs in Scythia. Bovines, quite present in alpine areas, were less commmon in the Mediterranean where they served mostly as work animals and their milk and its butter were associated with "barbarians" from the north. The ancient Romans were familiar with the cheese made from cow's milk eaten in the Empire's provinces beyond the alps but they preferred that of goats and sheep which were sometimes flavored with herbs and spices and conserved by smoking. This food was to lose favor in Italy during the early Middle Ages when for feudal lords and ladies it suggested rustic farmers, coarse mountain dwellers and uncouth shepherds: "peasants' food", but an acceptable substitute for game on the days when the Church prohibited meat. This disparaging attitude was also influenced by the fact that the puzzling process by which cheese was made, involving such mysterious phenomena as fermentation and mold, were not yet understood, nor were its nutritional qualities yet recognized; for example, the Salerno School of Medicine, the most important and authoritive fount of medical knowledge from antiquity to the 13th century, believed it could be healthy, but only in very small doses.

With the Renaissance, however, things changed in northern Italy. In addition to the usual small, soft, fresh "raw" sheep and goat cheeses, wealthy people began to eat large, hard, aged, "cooked"

"Annunciation to the Shepherds", affresco in the 12th cent. Church of San Peyre (St. Peter) attributed to anonymous Master of Stroppo: on a precipice (1080 mt.) in the Valle Maira, Stroppo was once a bustling commercial center, now prized for its landscape & tranquility

cow's milk cheese and their chefs began to use it in cooking. This was largely due to the rebirth of agriculture in the 12th century when the draining of swamps and the digging of irrigation canals in the Po River Plain substantially increased pasture lands: previously, grazing cows had lived mostly in high alpine meadows but now the prospering lowland farms run by monasteries, responsible for much of the land reclamation, made new area available. The change in bovine habitat from remote mountain mountain villages to the plains triggered cheese's entrance into the fledgling market economy that would soon permit the development of urban communities for the great quantities of milk these cows produced motivated the agrarian monks to find an alternative to the fresh cheese they normally made, which spoiled within a few days. Thus were born such inimitable hard examples as GRANA, or parmesan, and CASTELMAGNO: more complicated to make but easier to transport and preserve, they became a fundamental food for farmhands to take to the fields, and for soldiers, sailors and travelers. Hard cheese not only utilized and conserved milk, it was an ideal merchandise: in 1277, rounds of Castelmagno were used to pay rent for pasture lands belonging to the Marquis of Saluzzo.

Monk Making Cheese from fresco cycle "Scenes from Rural Monastic Life", attributed to Giovanni Mazzucco, late 1400's. Ex-Dominican Monastery in Bertini, near Roccaforte Mondovi (Cuneo)

A sign of cheese's new status is Summa lacticiniorm, the first printed book devoted to a single food –milk and milk products, especially cheese- by Pantaleone da Confienza, born near Vercelli, head physician at the Savoy Court for much of the second half of the 1400's and professor of medicine in Turin and Pavia. Published in Latin in Turin in 1477, it discusses the qualities of human's and animals' milk, how they are affected by climate and environment, how cheese is made, types of Italian and foreign cheeses –he had visited much of northern Europe- and finally treats more emotive factors: it was still believed that one's diet and digestion were influenced by the elements –air, water, fire, earth- and their corresponding properties – cold, damp, hot, dry- which produced the body's essential fluids –blood, phlegm, yellow bile (choler), black bile (melancholy). Pantaleone's description of the effects that eating cheese, and when best eaten, could have on different types of people seems quaintly unscientific but he clearly recognized its high nutritional value. While vestiges of medieval thought give this book an amusing, naive tone, it is a serious, scholarly work based on direct experience and observation, an example of the new interest in studying nature and the material world that would eventually replace the traditional scholasticism still dominant in intellectual circles.

Peasant Carrying Pannier, engraving by Giovenale Boetto (1604-1678). From Fossano, after working in Savigliano, in 1631 he was hired as Court Engineer & Architect for the Savoy Court. His architectural works can be seen, mostly in the province of Cuneo, but few of his printed works remain, many of which were done to commemorate political & military events, lavish official activities & theater performances. His realistic renderings of poor country folk introduced Caravaggesque qualities into the Piedmont's art. Figures such as this man were still occasinally seen in this Region 'til the 1950's. Royal Library, Turin

A second monograph, "Formaggiata di Sere Stentato al Serenissimo Re della Virtude", (a "nonsense" title, approximately: "cheese by Sir Suffering for the Royal Highness"), was written by Giulio Landi, a nobleman from Piacenza, first printed there in 1542. Motivated by the desire to promote the cheese from his native city which was beginning to be better known as PARMIGIANO, for the nearby city of Parma which also produced it, Landi emphasized its social and political value along with its gastronomic possibilities and his words are applicapable to other notable hard cheeses. He advised giving them as gifts to one's superiors, not only to make a good impression but to "open doors" that would otherwise remain shut; for him, cheese was the essential ingredient that gives soul and character to any food and makes for a general sense of well-being. "Formaggiata" was reprinted only twice (1572, 1601) but it was followed by other publications, mostly sonnets and poems, exalting cheese that make clear this food had found a secure place in the realm of aristocrats.

In addition to the usual round forms, square cheese began to be made which fit more easily into mules' saddlebags, faciliting transport from alpine meadows to the lowlands and they soon became a profitable commodity, exported, sold and traded at local and foreign markets. Methods of cheesemaking, however, changed very little over the centuries: the extremely precise details in "De re rusticae" (on farming) by Columella in the 1^t century are very similar to those in Pietro de' Crescenzi's "Ruralium commodorum libri" (on rural life), written 1300 years later which likewise remained valid a few hundred years. This art did not attract the interest of agrarians during the Enlightenment, but in the late 17-early 1800's, cows, their milk and what they ate began to be discussed: the excellent sweet alfalfa, clover and dandelions that were cultivated on the Val Padana's irrigated pastures and which grew wild on mountain meadows where the cows were transferred for the summer were recognized as fundamental for the unique flavors of the Piedmont's cheeses along with the cheesemakers' methods, based mostly on intuition, experience and a profound understanding of this activity. As Luigi Cattaneo wrote in his prize-winning work presented to the Realm of Lombardy-Veneto's Imperial Institute of Arts and Sciences in 1836 and published the following year, "Il Caseificio o la fabbricazione dei formaggi" (cheesemaking), cheesemakers needed acumen, common sense and a good memory and should be logical, quick and ready to deal with unforseen situations for nothing was written regarding their work. Some technical improvement came in the form of thermometers, proposed as early as 1785 –some 70 years after the German physicist Gabriel Daniel Fahrenheit perfected what Galileo had envisioned 100 years earlier- but not readily adopted since this advice was often repeated in books on related subjects, and Cattaneo again asserted their advantages. While cheesemaking has greatly benefitted from subsequent scientific progress and modern hygienic standards, nothing can replace practice and knowledge accumulated over time, aspects that are still very much a part of Piedmontese cheesemakers' techniques. Several factors determine the type and qualities of a cheese: the temperature to which the milk is heated before adding the, usually liquid, rennet, the speed of the curdling process, how the curds are broken, the pressing and salting, how long it ages before eaten and the environment in which this takes place.

The Piedmont is extraordinarily rich in cheese: virtually every part of the Region has at least one local example and they present an amazing array of shades –white, yellow, beige, brown- and forms, a word that shares its origins with the Italian FORMAGGIO, or cheese, as this food is made by putting milk in a container, or form, to solidify. Most of these cheeses are "handmade", using traditional methods and thus, unlike industrially produced ones, their quantity is limited and often depends on the time of year. Their excellence is seen in the fact that of the thirty Italian cheeses recognized as DOP, nine are Piedmontese. In 1992 the European Union established the designation known in Italy as DENOMINAZIONE DI ORIGINE PROTETTA, awarded to agricultural and food products possessing unique qualities derived from their natural environment and thus are authentic only when they come from that particular place: the neighboring valley is often different enough to be outside the defined area. This official recognition protects and maintains their quality

Dissodatrice
machine used to prepare soil for planting. Museum of Rural Life, Andrate (north of Ivrea) donated by Luciano Valpreda, Torre Canavese

and particular character and replaced the similar DOC
(DENOMINAZIONE DI ORIGINE CONTROLLATA) which a
few European countries began to use after World War II.

Several Piedmont cheeses are quite strong, they
smell more than other Italian cheeses and everything
about them, their form, color, rind, texture, consistency, odor, taste and aftertaste exudes individuality.
While used in making a few traditional dishes, these
cheeses are best eaten on their own and more than in
other parts of Italy, a separate course is often dedicated to them both in restaurants and private
homes. In many places fresh fruit is a common accompaniment to cheese, along with crackers and
bread, although Italians eat little of the latter, con-
suming it instead with a fork and knife. More unusual, but I was quickly won over, is the
Piedmontese custom of combining this food with
local honey and marmelades made from dandelions, chestnuts, blueberries, onions, grape
must etc., the silverware making it possible to dip a piece of cheese into these jel-
lied preserves, sweet enough to tem-
per the pungent taste of the strong-
est ones without overpowering the
milder ones. This union creates
extremely interesting and delicious contrasts of flavor and texture, more intense than with
fresh fruit, that are further
enchanced by the Region's full-
bodied wines.

The artisan aspect of alpine
cheese production not only insures
their high quality, it also helps pro-
tect and preserve the Piedmont's beautiful landscape, and the exodus that depopulated
much of Italy's mountainous areas after World War II is, in some places, being reversed. A

new appreciation of traditional products typical of these often isolated communities and easier communication between them and the lowlands has meant that, in spite of difficulties and sacrifices involved in dedicating oneself to making "old-fashioned" cheese, some young people are committing themselves to reviving this art. Maintaining fertile pastures and keeping water pure, both necessary for having healthy cows and good milk and cheese also helps conserve the natural environment and thus these villages give much more than gastronomic pleasures.

Numerous publications offer information about Italian cheeses. However, I confess that the written word regarding this food does not excite my fantasy the way reading certain recipes can conjure up a vicarious feast. I find it difficult to imagine the reality of something "...medium fat, of a hard consistency which when young is fine and delicate tasting with a thin, smooth, yellowish rind that, with aging, becomes intense and sharp, its rind rough and darkened". Only after eating Castelmagno of differing ages does such a description make sense, the words recalling its remarkable flavor and consistency, its tendency to crumble, the way it seems to dissolve in one's mouth, so different from what might be expected from such a strong, "virile" cheese. While the Piedmont's hard cheeses are very distinctive in

Cheese Counter,
Indoor Market,
Cuneo

123

appearace, soft, fresh ones, to an ignorant eye, look rather similar: plump, whitish discs, from 10 to 15 centimeters in diameter and from 2 to 4 in height, 'tho there are singular exceptions such as the pancake-like Robiola di Cocconato. But, their anonymous physique is deceiving and hides the intriguing fact that, within a few days, even these young ones "age": their soft smooth exterior may get a bit thicker, bumpy or darker, their mild taste gets a hint of sharpness, their odor more pungent, and what was moist, creamy and easy to spread is equally easy to slice.

If the number of essentials for making something were a sign of its worth, cheese would seem rather unimportant. The requisites for making artisan, non-industrial, hard Italian cheese are quite limited: milk from cows, goats or sheep; rennet, usually liquid, from the lining of a calf's stomach and containers for mixing it with the milk to produce curds; a few simple utensils for stirring, skimming and breaking the curds; cloth for straining the curdled mass and space for working it by hand; molds for forming the cheese which is subsequently pressed, salted (absorbed by the cheese, it acts as a preservative and antiseptic), sometimes pressed again and then aged. Even without understanding the subtleties of such processes as heating the milk, adding the rennet and breaking the curds at exactly the right moment, one marvels at the variety of cheeses these standard ingredients and procedures create and admires the knowledge and skill cheesemakers must possess to practice this art. The aging, for example, requires close attention as the temperature and humidity of the environment where it takes place must be monitored, the cheeses must be turned over regularly, their rinds scraped, brushed or washed for a year or more before they are ready to eat. Since most of the Piedmont's FORMAGGI are made using these traditinal methods, they have personality, character, impossible to maintain with large scale production.

Words, however, are feeble and inadequate. The only way to understand these cheeses is to eat them, admittedly not always a simple undertaking since some of them are best found in the area where they are made and

Spannarola, or skimmer, wooden utensil for skimming cream off the milk when making cheese. Museum of the City of Cuneo

production is limited and often influenced by season. For cheeselovers, and non, I have no hesitation in recommending a trip dedicated to trying the outstanding examples this Region offers which, in addition to its gastronomic interest, takes one to numerous beautiful, scenic, tucked-away places usually not part of tourist itineraries but well worth discovering. While anything that looks tempting should be tried, the following pages describe, in alphabetical order, some of the Piedmont's most notable, but not necessarily most famous, cheeses.

From **"Family Banquet To Celebrate A Birth"** (1750), pen & wash drawing by Pietro Domenico Olivero (1679-1755), from Turin. The simple fare includes pieces of cheese on the cupboard shelf. Royal Library, Turin

BRA *Named for the city that was once the principal marketplace for cheese made in the mountainous areas of the province of Cuneo, alpine Bra and that of the plains were among its most prised merchandise: made predominantly from cow's milk, with a small quantity of sheep's and goat's milk, they are both DOP. Alpine Bra dates back to the 1300's and before Parmigiano became Italy's "national" grating cheese in the 1900's, when aged, it was the Piedmont's and Liguria's usual grating cheese. While the same techniques are used for making both types, the equipment in the mountains is more rustic, entailing more manual labor and the milk used is almost always from cows of the Piedmontese breed, nourished on fresh local forage.*

SIZE: Diameter, 30-40 cm. Height, 7-9 cm. Weight, 6-8 kg.

CASTELMAGNO *Born in the narrow, steep valley of the torrent Grana and named for the village that sits at an altitude of 1800 meters on the road, now paved, that follows this water's path, Castelmagno has been made for at least 800 years. It belongs to the family of ERBORINATI (from ERBA, or grass) which includes such cheeses as Gorgonzola, called so because of the blue-green mold they develop. The damp environment of the cave-like spaces carved in the Val Grana's rock where Castelmagno is aged facilitates this growth*

Campomolino: *Six kilometers east & 650 mt. below Castelmagno, this remote hamlet is the municipal seat of this alpine area, composed of a few sparsely inhabited settlements hidden among forests & high fertile pastures*

126

which, for devotees, greatly adds to the already pronounced, inimitable flavor of the whiter, younger DOP cheese. Production of this mostly cow's milk cheese –a bit of sheep's and goat's milk may be added- is very limited.

SIZE: Diameter, 15-25 cm. Height, 15-20 cm. Weight, 2-7 kg.

FONTINA
Not Piedmontese but, rather, from neighboring Valle d'Aosta: due to their vicinity this cheese is very present in Piedmontese cuisine. Made from the milk of Valdostana cows, it often has a few holes or "eyes. Since it melts very well, becoming smooth and creamy, it is perhaps more appreciated "cooked" than raw. This DOP cheese is recognized by its trademark, the profile of a mountain and its name enclosed within a circle.

SIZE: Diameter, 30-45 cm. Height, 7-10 cm. Weight, 8-18 kg.

MURAZZANO
Originally made only from sheep's milk, today it usually contains up to 40% cow's. Ready to eat within seven days, if this soft, delicate tasting DOP cheese is aged a few months it develops a slight rind and its flavor deepens. Named for a town in the Langhe where it is made, its somewhat nondescript circular form is distinguished by the triangular white paper with blue writing that wraps it. Its smooth consistency may be marked with tiny "eyes".

SIZE: Diameter, 10-15 cm. Height, 3-4 cm. Weight, 300-400 gr

RASCHERA
Some goat's and sheep's milk may be added to this basically cow's milk cheese produced around Monte Mongioie in the southern part of the province of Cuneo: the particular area, called Ruscaira, and a lake there, called Raschera, give it its name. Semi-soft, it may be round or four-sided with rounded corners. That made at the foot of the 2630 meter mountain is DOP, identified by a green label; the yellow-labled alpine Raschera is particularly prized for its characteristic flavor, rendered by the fragrant grasses eaten by cows grazing at over 900 meters. Its production, which a few years ago was decreasing is now picking up, a fact that would please the Piedmontese Ludovico Bertoldi, physician to the Dukes of Savoy, were he alive today: in his annotations to the book "Regole della sanità et natura dei cibi" (rules of health and the nature of food) by

the Sienese Ugo Benzo, printed in Turin in 1620, Bertoldi specifically refers to the cheese made near Mondovì in the region called "Ruschiara".

SIZE: Diameter, 35-40 cm, if square, side =40cm. Height, 7-12 cm. Weight, 5-8 kg.

RICOTTA

Ricotta is more a byproduct than an actual cheese: it is made by reheating residue whey produced when making cheese, hence its name, meaning "recooked". In Piedmontese it is SEIRASS, from the Latin seracium, meaning tight, squeezed, perhaps a reference to its being hung in a linen bag to drain excess liquid. It may be made from cow's, sheep's or goat's whey and be round, cone-shaped or cylindrical in addition to the typical upside-down basket form. This soft, white, creamy cheese is produced throughout the Piedmont and is sometimes lightly smoked to preserve it but it is only in the remote mountain valleys near Pinerolo where the Waldenses, the followers of the 12th century religious dissenter Peter Waldo, found refuge after fleeing southern France, that the unique SEIRASS DEL FEN is made from the whey of

From "**Adoration of The Shepherds**", terra cotta statue by Gaudenzio Ferrari, 1514, from Holy Mount of Varallo, Chapel VII. When the Tu conquered the Holy Land in 1453, it becam difficult for Christians to continue making pilgrimages there, a problem partly resolved building a "New Jerusalem" closer to home. Vatican's opposition to the Reformation in mid-1500's added impetus to the project begun in the late 1400's above the city of Varallo: 600 life-sized (& greater) terra & wooden statues, often sumptuously cl plus animals, present the life of Christ chapels richly decorated with fresco filled with 4,000 painted figures. Tl to the collaboration of leading artis architects the dramatic, but realist emotional intensity of the scenes captures even non-believers. The chapel was built in 1737.

TOMA CHEESE. Ricotta should be eaten fresh and its producers need quick access to markets, a requisite denied to residents of the isolated VALLI VALDESI where the lack of roads made it difficult to descend from alpine pastures while their SEIRASS was still fresh and so it was salted, like hard cheese, and aged for a few months. About three weeks before going down to be sold, the forms were wrapped in hay, or FIENO, FEN in Piedmontese, which protected them from flies and jostling in the saddlebags of the mules carrying them. Transport has improved but this singular method of treating Ricotta continues, appreciated now for aesthetic reasons and the delicate fragrance the hay gives.

I once bought some ricotta from a farmer-shepherd who set up a table near the Shrine of Oropa (north of Biella) to sell the few cheeses he made from his sheep. It was extraordinary & as he assured me, by covering it with a veil of olive oil it kept for a few weeks in the refrigerator. Thus, do not hesitate to take advantage of similar opportunities.

Goat from **"Dintorni di Rivara"** (near Rivara), 1861, oil on canvas by local artist Carlo Pittara (1835-1891). This Canavese village was home to the famous Rivara Group of painters that from 1860-1880 spent summers there. Their opposition to the current academic, provincial style in vogue brought innovation & a new freedom to Piedmontese art. GAM Museum, Turin

ROBIOLA

A variety of fresh cheeses are called Robiola: made from cow's and/or goat's milk, a bit of sheep's may also be added. The most famous is ROBIOLA DI ROCCAVERANO, from the provinces of Alessandria and Asti and while it may contain up to 85% cow's milk, the one that is 100% goat's is Italy's only DOP goat cheese. The village of Roccaverano lends its name to cheese produced over an extendd area but it is the center for ROBIOLA DEL BEC, made only in October and November when nannygoats are in heat and mate with billy-goats, BEC in Piedmontese, and their milk becomes extremely rich and tasty. People who have a goat or two make Robiola, called FURMAGETTA in the local dialect, for private consumption; a cooperative just outside Roccaverano sells local cheeses and sometimes have a slightly aged pure goat's one, scrumptious grated or cut.

In the first decades of the 20th century the Piedmont had more goats than other regions of northern and central Italy but this is no longer the case and much less of this cheese is made today. Goats not only produce more milk than other mammals with respect to their size and weight —cows render 10 to 15 times their weight, goats, 15 to 20- (thus their nickname, "cow of the poor"), it is also the most nutricious and digestible, and being virtually immune to tuberculosis bacteria, it need not be pasturized. In addition, its unique chemical composition makes it particularly invigorating and stimulating, especially for older people. It has been suggested that the predominance of goat's milk in ancient Mediterranean societies helps explain their extraordinary vitality, creativity and artistic and intellectual achievements: from a hormonal aspect, cow's milk is neutral and tranquil while goat's is dynamic and active and milk is recognized as being a determining factor in the development of a people's character. Goats, however, have attracted much less scientific interest than bovines, perhaps due to these very differences. The latter adapt much better to a controlled environment, to living in barns and stalls and thus are easier to study than the free-spirited, sometimes rambunctious CAPRE, whose name in Italian shares the same Latin origins as the words capricious and caprice, descriptive of this animal.

SIZE: Robiola di Roccaverano: Diameter, 10-14 cm. Height, 4-5 cm. Weight, 400 gr.
Robiola del Bec: Diameter, 12-16 cm. Height, 6-8 cm. Weight, 300-600 gr.

TOMA

Usually a rather large, alpine cow's milk cheese, one finds many different examples of Toma throughout the Piedmont as well as in the Valle d'Aosta, Sicily and France. In the Piedmont they are normally from 10 to 40 cm. in diameter, 5 to 15 cm. high and weigh from 200 grams to 11 kg.: their rinds range from yellowish-white to dark red-brown, their consistency is compact, solid but elastic, their interior a warm straw color with occasional "eyes" and several are DOP, distinguished by a round white paper label with blue, red and green markings. One of the most notable of these comes from the Ossola area in northern Piedmont which extends to the Swiss borber; called BETTLEMATT or OSSOLANO, like other hard cheeses born in medieval monasteries its history goes back some thousand years. Its limited production and remote geographic location have kept it less known and the hardships of mountain life, which became increasingly unacceptable in the face of modern comforts available in cities and towns, meant that many shepheds and cheesemakers abandoned that environment, thus reducing the already small quantity of this Toma. Moreover, its physical similarity to Swiss gruyere and the variety of names for it often made it difficult to identify. Bettlematt, which in the local dialect means "pasture of the chamois antelope", is made from the milk of cows grazing at from 1300 to 2200 meters above sea level. Not surprisingly, it is quite expensive and sold mostly in gourmet food shops while most other Toma cheeses are available at all types of cheese counters. For mountain dwellers, Toma was an essential part of their very limited diet, eaten with bread – usually rye, and baked but once a year, in November, in quantity to last 12 months-, potatoes, polenta and for very special occasions, with TAJARIN made of buckwheat flour.

TOMINO

As the diminuitive suffix implies, this is a small cheese, literally "little Toma", but the name is a misnomer: TOMINI are fresh cheeses, very white, usually of goat's milk, 'tho a notable sheep's milk one comes from the Langhe. While they may be aged –their mild taste and odor get stronger- they may also be conserved in olive oil with black or hot red pepper to make TOMINI ELETTRICI, called so for the "electric" shock this spice gives to the tongue.

BROSS

One of the Piedmont's most intriguing cheeses, Bross could be described as a born-again milk product. Also called Bros, Brussu, Bruz, Bruzzu, and Buzzu, it is fermented cheese, a miracle of recycling: very strong in taste and smell, its name is thought to derive from the verb BRUCIARE, to burn. Though said to have been "invented" by shepherds in the Langhe, as Luciano Gibelli wrote in his beautiful compendium of objects and customs of Piedmontese rural society with the equally beautiful title, "Memorie di cose, prima che scenda il buio" (memories of things, before darkness falls), similar concoctions exist in much of the Region's mountainous areas. It no doubt comes from the historic need to use everything, throw nothing away; in this case, all scraps of cheese and its rind not suited for chewing, melting or grating are cut or mashed as finely as possible, put in a terra cotta, glass or wooden container, then covered and left in a cool place. After a few days, a bit of GRAPPA or crushed black or hot red pepper is added. After a week, the contents are mashed to a smooth consistency, covered and put in a cool place 'til fermentation begins and then left undisturbed in a warmer place for 30-45 days to become creamy, fragrant and piquant. While any leftover cheese may be used, goat's and sheep's are best but today, no longer made from scraps, Robiola and Tomino are recommended, especially if aged three months, in which case they may be grated. For those who prefer not to make Bross, jars of it can be bought in gourmet shops and cheese markets. Bross can be spread on toasted bread or polenta and is usually eaten at the end of a meal, accompanied by wine, but is also a good snack for those who like very strong, pronounced flavors. It could be described as an "acquired taste".

Shrine of San Chiaffredo, near Saluzzo, from "Descrizioni dei santuarii del Piemonte" (descriptions of Piedmont's holy shrines) by Giovanni Reycend, published in Turin (1822-25) & dedicated to the Duke of Savoy & King of Sardinia, Carlo Felice. Virtually in the shadow of Monviso, San Chiaffredo (1417mt.), as Reycend wrote, was at the end of a road that eventually became almost too steep for mules: he calculated 45 minutes by foot from nearby Crissolo (1318 mt.), one of the preferred starting points for climbing the famous mountain. His 2 vol. work is not for tourists but, rather, is a guide for those seeking religious inspiration. The drawings, "from life", by M. Nicolosino were engraved by Arghinenti, about whom nothing is known. Marciana Library, Venice

131

Chocolate & Sweets
Cioccolato e Dolci

Turin is famous for numerous reasons: for example, it is the home of JUVENTUS, Italy's most famous soccer team and the beloved one called TORO, the Italian auto industry was born there and from 1563 to 1865 it was the principal residence of this country's royal family. With the rest of the Piedmont it played a leading role in uniting the entire peninsula and was the capital of the newly proclaimed Italian nation from 1861 to 1865, which then moved to Florence and, in 1871, to Rome. Important as these distinctions are, however, it enjoys yet another: Turin has always been this country's chocolate capital, renowned not only for this scrumptious food but also as the training ground where some of Europe's most famous CIOCCOLATIERI apprenticed this art. Many of the city's pastry and sweet shops, from elegant, historic CAFFE' and confectioneries to neighborhood bars offer a variety of homemade chocolates, sold by the piece, to savor immediately or take away, all sharing almost 500 years of history.

Chocolate is made from the seeds of the cacao tree, native to the equatorial regions of the Americas. It probably first grew in the forests and

Piazza Castello, *Turin:*
Palazzo Madama, Tower & Mole Antonelliana. Founded by Augustus in 28 B.C. as a settlement for army veterans, Turins's original orthogonal street plan of a Roman CASTRUM is one of few remaining signs of its ancient past. Two polygonal towers mark the site of the Pretorian Gate that became part of the fortified castle of the Acaja in the 1300's, later modified into Palazzo Madama, named for the title "Madama Reale" adopted by the Savoy duchesses in the 1600's. Its baroque facade (1718-1721) by Sicilian architect Filippo Juvarra was built for the French mother of Vittorio Amedeo II. The Mole Antonelliana, by Alessandro Antonelli, begun in 1863, finished in 1897, (165.50 mt.), houses the National Cinema Museum.

132

basins of the Amazon and Orinoco Rivers, then spread throughout that area and began to be cultivated some 3,000 years ago in Tabasco, in Mexico. Since the 19ᵗʰ century it also thrives in Africa but its very specific environment limits its existence. Cacao grows between the 22° parallels North and South, from 30 to 300 meters above sea level, with temperatures from 20 to 35°C. It needs abundant, well-distributed rain (but heavy downpours are damaging), constant high humidity and deep fertile soil. As wind and direct sun are harmful, fastgrowing shade trees, like banana, are often planted to protect the cacao saplings which belong to the family Sterculiaceae, a group of tropical trees and shrubs whose name derives from the Latin stercus, meaning animal dung, suggested by their dark brown seeds. At five years of age, trees begin to produce elongated, tapering brilliant red-yellow-gold fruit, about 18 cm.long and 8 cm.wide. A hard, ribbed and bumpy shell surrounds a slightly sour, white mucilagenous pulp which envelops from 30 to 50 little oval seeds: arranged in five tightly-packed overlapping rows –a miracle of order and design- they contain fat, water, starch, celluose, minerals, ash and the alkaloids theobromine and caffeine. Although cacao trees always have some flowers or fruit, which grow directly from the trunk and not on branches, harvesting takes place only twice a year, during the solstices when the dry and rainy seasons begin. The fruits' form, size, weight, color and seeds may vary but they all belong to the same species; their diversity lies in where they grow, such as Caracas, Trinidad, the African Gold Coast etc.

The word chocolate, CIOCCOLATO in Italian, comes from CHOCOLATL-CACAUTL, which in Nahuatl, the language of Mexican and Central American Indians, means money for these people used cacao beans as coins, a practice continued into the early 1900's by the Mayas in Guatemala. Thus, when Europeans first saw this plant in the 1500's, they called it "money tree". CACAUTL was also the name of the "bitter water", the hot, dark, dense beverage that by 600 B.C. both the Maya and Aztec Indians were making from their "coins". For them, the tree was of divine origin, from paradise, and the drink it produced was sacred and symbolized the earth's fertility. It was drunk only during religious ceremonies or by

Cacao, engraving from "Storie delle Piante Forestiere" (history of foreign plants) printed in Milan in 1791, illustrated by Benedetto & Gaudenzio Bordiga, from Varallo, near Biella, text by unnamed authors. Famous for his geographic & topographic works, Gaudenzio was Chief Engineer for the Italian military & professor of art.

Il Cacao

important people on special occasions as depicted on pre-Columbian vase and tomb paintings and explains the scientific name the 18th century Swedish botanist Karl von Linné, or Linnaeus, gave it: Theobroma cacao, food or drink of the gods, may also have been influenced by his great fondness for this beverage. The Indians also recognized CACAUTL'S therapeutic properties and used cacao butter to treat burns, snake bites and to cauterize wounds and is still used in the pharmaceutical and cosmetic industries.

To make CACAUTL the Indians separated the seeds from the white pulp around them, which made a pleasing drink if diluted in water, and left them out in the sun a few days to dry and ferment a bit to bring out their flavor. Then they roasted them, an essential process that enhances the taste and aroma of many seeds and nuts and releases their fat content. Next, the seeds were ground into a thick dark paste to which were added vanilla, spices —including hot pepper- and sometimes, cornmeal. Left to cool and harden, this paste was pounded 'til powdery, then mixed with hot water and beaten to a foamy consistency: before drinking CACAUTL, they poured it back and forth several times from one container held high up to another below in order to increase its frothiness. This was the essence of the drink that was to have great economic and social effects on Europe in the 17th and 18th centuries.

Ferdinand Columbus, Christopher's son, wrote that his father saw cacao seeds on the island of Guanaja, near Honduras, during his fourth and final voyage to the New World in 1502 but Europeans seemingly had no direct contact with this plant 'til 1519 when the Spanish general and explorer, Hernando Cortez, entered Mexico where the Aztec Emperor, Montezuma II, served him and his officers a mysterious, dense, steaming brown drink in gold goblets that the invaders found disagreeably spicey and bitter 'tho cacao, and vanilla, were among the treasures they presented to King Charles V when they returned to Spain in 1526. Similarly, as Girolamo Benzoni, the Milanese adventurer who participated in several expeditions to the New World wrote in "La storia del mondo nuovo" (history of the New World) printed in Venice in 1565, he drank the strange beverage only if wine and water were lacking but admitted it was refreshing and satisfying and, moreover, did not cause drunkeness. Other Italians, and Europeans, were more critical, to the point of finding the mere sight of the foamy fat floating on the liquid's surface nauseating.

CACAUTL remained an interesting but ignored oddity in Spain until someone there prepared the Indians' drink and instead of the usual spices, added another precious ingredient, sugar —unknown in the New World- creating a concoction that quickly won favor among the local aristocracy. Like cacao, sugar entered Europe via Spain. Sugar cane is native to India – the Sanscrit word for it, SAKHARA, also meaning sand, is the source for the words sugar and the Italian ZUCCHERO- from where it spread to the Persian Gulf and then to Egypt, where it was first purified and refined. The Arabs brought it from North Africa to Spain when they invaded that country in the 8th century and, like spices, became a very profitable commodity with the revival of trade in the Middle Ages. It was expensive, used more for medicinal than culinary purposes, a situation that changed after 1493 when Columbus brought sugar cane from the Canary Islands to Santo Domingo and by 1530 Spanish-owned sugar plantations worked by African slaves were exporting this luxury item to Europe. News of the Spanish court's new sweet drink leaked to the outside world thanks to merchants, missionaries, travelers and political events. In 1557 the Duke of Savoy Emanuele Filiberto, while serving as Governor General for the Spanish King, Philip II, defeated the French in the Battle of St.Quentin, a spectacular victory that brought his family new territory, power and prestige and the close ties established with Spain are thought to have facilitated the introduction of cacao into Italy. Six years later, France's 25 year occupation of Turin ended: Emanuele Filiberto transferred the Savoy's capital there from Chambery, Italian replaced French as the city's official language and CACAUTL began to be made. The ready acceptance of this drink in the Piedmont was perhaps influenced by the fact that the Duke's successor, his son Carlo Emanuele I, was married to Philip II's daughter, who had drunk chocolate at the Spanish court. The King of France, Louis XIII, was also married to a princess of Spanish origin, as was his son, Louis XIV, but the foreign beverage did not generate interest among the French 'til the second half of the 1600's by which time Turin had become Europe's leading chocolate producer – about 350 kilograms a day- most of which was exported to Austria, Germany and Switzerland. Hot chocolate made its public debut in 1678 when the CIOCCOLATIERE Giovanni Antonio Ari received royal permission to sell cups of it in Turin, a privilege he held for six years.

CACAUTL had lost its sacred connotation but its consumption was still very limited: it was, like the sugar used to sweeten it, a luxury, drunk only by the wealthy, men and women alike but, it seems,

ships
from woodcut map of Brazil by Giacomo Gastaldi in Giambattista Ramusio's "Delle navigationi et viaggi", V.III, printed in Venice, 1556. Gastaldi(1500-1566), from Villafranca Piemonte, was Italy's, & one of Europe's, greatest 16th cent. mapmakers. He spent much of his life in Venice, working as an engineer, surveyor & cartographer for the Republic. His edition of Ptolemy, his maps of the World, Europe, Asia, Africa etc. were the basis for many subsequent maps 'tho his contribution was often not acknowledged. He always signed his works, many of which were milestones in this art, with his name followed by "PIEMONTESE". His maps relied heavily on Ramusio's collection of original descriptions of places & their cultures: the 3 volumes of "Navigationi" are the first examples of a systematic organization of "travel literature". Marciana Library, Venice

not children, in private homes and in the "chocolate houses" that opened in cities large and small. Shortly after 1750 it returned to the New World, where North American colonists began drinking the hot beverage born on that continent, but introduced to them thanks to Europeans. The Indians' spiritual ritual was thus replaced by a social one, as depicted in paintings and prints and gave birth to a growing array of cookies and biscuits created just for dunking. Not only were artists inspired by it: poets exalted the drink's aphrodisiac powers, clerics pondered over whether it could be drunk during Lent, or because a liquid, when fasting; physians described its restorative effects and philosophers sought to distinguish the differences between chocolate and food. It was also the impetus for the production of a variety of culinary accessories: elegant silver pots and spoons and delicate, ornate porcelain cups and saucers were made, many now valued by museums and antique collectors.

It is interesting that, as extraordinary as Turin's chocolate is, the city's famous version of the hot drink also contains coffee. Originally called BAVAREISA, it was a combination of milk, coffee, hot chocolate and sweet syrup which in the 1700's was renamed BICERIN, from BICCHIERE, or drinking glass, used instead of a ceramic cup. Unlike the BAVAREISA, it was not a fixed preparation: the steaming milk, coffee and chocolate were served separately and mixed to one's personal taste, usually accompanied by cookies. It was enormously popular and Turin was called BICERINOPOLI: normally it was drunk before noon by people from all walks of life in the city's numerous cafés, some of which were famous for the many national and foreign newspapers one could read in them, facilitated by the introduction of gas lighting in the 1840's. These cafés served social and philosophical purposes: they were a refuge for political exiles from other Italian cities, a place to meet, to discuss and exchange ideas about liberty and unification and they played a vital role in the development of the Risorgimento movement. By the late 1800's the BICERIN was rarely drunk and it all but disappeared with World War I; a few cafés still serve it but, like the BAVAREISA, it is already mixed.

Like other foods that once only the rich could afford, such as pasta, white bread and spices, chocolate eventually became "democratized", though until 1828, the only form of it most people knew was the warm beverage. In that year, Conrad Van Houten, in Holland, used an hydraulic press to extract about 60% of the paste's cocoa butter, dried the rest and pulverized it to make powdered chocolate, eliminating the oily layer normally skimmed off CIOCCOLATA before drinking it: its presence may explain why the Indians liked it frothy and is probably why the lids of antique chocolate pots have a tiny hole for inserting a utensil to sir the contents, distinguishing them from similar teapots. Numerous other changes were in the making that would revolutionize the confectionary world, some being a direct result of the fact that an economic alternative to sugar cane was being developed.

Beta vulgaris L.

In the 1600's it was understood that beets produce a sweet syrup but how to convert it into sugar crystals was not discovered 'til the second half of the 1700's, in Silesia, where attempts to eliminate importing this expensive commodity led to large scale cultivation of sugar beets, *Beta vulgaris L.*, and the first sugar factory opened there in 1801. Related efforts took place in the Piedmont where starting in the late 1700's, grapes, corn stalks, mulberries, apples, chestnuts and even pea pods were tried as a source of sugar, albeit with limited success. Political events, however, provided new motivation for such research. Conflicts between England and France led the former to impose the Blockade that in 1806 prevented the Continent from importing, among other things, West Indian sugar and Europe's interest in beets increased, even after the block was lifted. Experiments with the plants just mentioned were abandoned: in 1836 the renowned Piedmontese botanist, Matteo Bonafous, Director of Turin's Botanical Garden, presented a project for growing beets, and the funds for it, to the city's Royal Agrarian Society, of which he was a member. It was approved: chemists and farmers selected seeds from Belgium and Silesia, where the sweetest varieties of beets grew, planted them in Moncalieri, near Turin, and the industrial production of sugar was soon underway. This cultivation, much encouraged by Italy's greatest 19th century statesman, Camillo Cavour, spread to the Canavese and Stura areas and sugar began to enter the Piedmont's kitchens.

As sugar became cheaper and more accessible, so did certain foods made with it. Sweets continued to be reserved for special occasions well into the 1900's but the availability of this ingredient facilitated confectioners and pastry cooks to experiment and expand their repertoire. Sweet hard chocolate was first made in England in 1847 when the paste, sugar and cocoa butter were combined to make a solid piece; in 1876, in Switzerland, the addition of condensed milk gave birth to milk chocolate and Italy also contributed to these innovations. In 1860, decreased cacao production, and thus higher prices, made it difficult to obtain. To make what there was go further, a Turin CIOCCOLATIERE added ground roasted filberts to his cacao, creating a new chocolate with a remarkably smooth and creamy texture and named it GIANDUIA, a word of great political and cultural significance.

Conflicts with then French had continued over the centuries: in 1802 they annexed the Piedmont and hostility toward them was felt beyond the battlefields. In 1808, two puppeteers from the province of Asti made a marionette and named it Gironi, but the critical comments about Napolean that came from its mouth and its name, too similar to that of the Emperor's brother, Jerome, King of Westphalia, caused problems. Gironi's anti-French sentiments were too blatant for the foreign occupiers and after a performance of "Artabano I, Re del mondo con Girolamo suo confidante, Re per

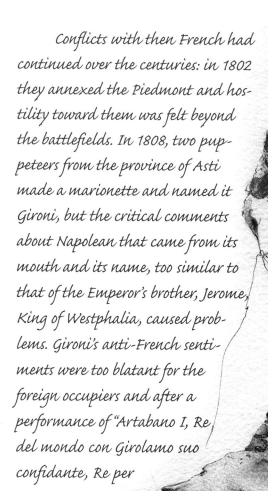

women but he began to reveal anti-French sentiment and a sense of independence, becoming

combinazione" (Artabano I, King of the world with his confidant Girolamo, King by chance) the puppeteers had to leave Turin and could return only if Gironi disappeard. Thus, a new character was born named GIAN D'LA DOIA, or DUIA, a Piedmont dialect form of GIOVANNI DEL BOCALE or "John of the Jug", that popular speech shortened to GIANDUIA, dressed in a brown jacket with red trim, short green trousers, red socks and the typical 18th century three-cornered hat over a pig-tailed wig. At first, Gianduia was a simple, good-hearted, high-spirited lover of wine and

honorable, virtuous and patriotic. The wooden doll became a symbol of national pride for all levels of society and after the House of Savoy returned to power in 1814, the puppeteers were invited to perform for the Royal Court.

Gianduia, 19th cent. marionette.
Lupi Marionette Museum-
Gianduia Theater, Turin

No longer just a marionette, Gianduia became the mouthpiece for the Piedmont's political convictions. More than Italy's other famous charicature theatrical figures like Naples' Pulcinella, Bergamo's Arlecchino, Rome's Rugantino or Florence's Stenterello, Turin's is associated with social issues and moved from the stage to the printed page. By the 1840's Gianduia was being immortalized in articles and satirical vignettes in papers supporting the liberation and unification of Italy as proposed by the Risorgimento movement. But, as winsome, beloved and significant as this figure was both artistically and politically, much of its fame today is due to the cacao shortage mentioned above. In 1865 the Caffarel-Prochet-Gay chocolate makers in Turin used the filbert-Gianduia mixture created five years earlier to make a new candy and named it GIANDUIOTTO, once again in honor of the patriotic puppet: Italy would soon become a single state and nationalistic feelings were particularly fervent in the Piedmont. Gianduia's popularity even made a marionette's dream come true for he was transformed into a live theatrical character and continued to be a symbol in the fight for freedom: Italy's first antifascist newspaper, founded in Turin in 1924, was named "Il codino rosso" (red pigtail) after his coiffure. Historical events are probably not mused over while a Gianduiotto is voluptuously melting in one's mouth, but this candy's distinctive triangular form, inspired by the puppet's three-cornered hat, is a lasting tribute to its political importance.

Gianduiotti traditionally wrapped in gold foil, several chocolate houses make them, each using a slightly different secret recipe

The confusion caused by the use of three different words to refer to the nut of the European hazel tree prompted the American Joint Committee on Horticulture Nomenclature, in 1942, to choose filbert as the official name for this member of the birch family but, despite bureaucratic decisions, hazelnut is still common: cobnut is rarely used. Filbert derives from the Old Norman French name Philibert: St. Philibert, who died in 684, was an abbot and founded monasteries and convents in France and since his feast day is August 20th, during the period when this nut is gathered, it was named in his honor. The Italian NOCCIOLO – the tree- and NOCCIOLA –the nut- come from the Latin nux, or nut. It was once thought that the NOCCIOLO came to Italy from Asia Minor in the 1st century B.C., brought by the Roman general Lucullus on returning after his victory over Mithridates, King of Pontus on the Black Sea, where it was intensely cultivated. But, archeological and geological remains show it is indigenous here and was a valuable food since the Stone Age. Small, robust, pointed leaves surround the nut's shell: its scientific name, Corylus, from the Greek KORYS, meaning helmet, refers to this double protective covering. Nonetheless, it is cracked open without difficulty making the nut and its highly nutricious, easily digested oil very accessible. Corylus avellanus, the most common variety in Italy, was named for the area of Avellino, in Campania, where this country's cultivation began during antiquity and continues to flourish. Considering it is a Mediterranean plant, associated with southern Italy, Sicily, Sardinia, Spain and Turkey, it is curious that what many judge the best of all filberts grows in the Piedmont, though it accounts for very little of the world's production. This tree adapts well to a diversity of soil types but prefers hilly ground and moist, breezy mild weather: vulnerable to cold, winter frost and strong, chill dry winds are damaging. In a sort of agricultural miracle, the climate, soil, terrain and exposure around the cities of Asti and Cuneo, albeit in northern Italy, have been skillfully exploited to create a unique, very tasty variety of filbert called TONDA GENTILE DELLE LANGHE (sweet sphere of the Langhe).

Resembling both a tree and a shrub, this plant has anywhere from three to ten slender, smooth "stems" instead of a single trunk and its leaf-laden branches extend out and up as high as three meters into a graceful fan-like shape. Parallel rows of widely-spaced trees accentuate the irregularity of the Langhe landscape, making pleasing patterns as they follow the slopes and curves of the gray-beige soil. The town of Cortemilia is the center of this cultivation which began in the 1800's in an attempt to increase the scarce quantities gathered from the trees that grew wild; NOCCIOLI were also an important substitute for the grapes that were being destroyed by an epidemic of parasites and fungi —some of Italy's best wines come from these hillsides- and since they survive at altitudes where vineyards cannot, more land could be productive. The invention of GIANDUIA and GIANDUIOTTO in the 1860's stimulated this cultivation, later favored by the growing use of filberts in cakes, cookies and nougats which not only brought fame and revenue to this area, but also provided more work opportunities and helped combat the depopulation of the Alte Langhe, as occurred in many parts of rural Italy in the 1900's. In addition, this farming safeguards this precious landscape from neglect and abandon.

Tonda Gentile delle Langhe

When the TONDA GENTILE is ripe it drops from its branch –it need not be picked-making a soft plopping sound as it hits the ground, carpeting it with smooth little brown balls. Until the early 1990's they were still gathered by hand: in the second half of August migrant farm workers, housewives, students...all got down on their knees to separate the nuts from their leaves but the invention of machines designed for this and other phases of the filbert's life cycle changed this and made it possible to extend cultivation over more and steeper terrain. In Cortemilia in the late 1800's the first machines for shelling, measuring, selecting and roasting the TONDA GENTILE were created, transforming the raw nut into a ready-to-use ingredient for the food industry and subsequent improvements regarding its gathering, drying and grinding led to an even higher quality product. The flavor and aroma of most seeds and nuts are enchanced by roasting but this process has a particularly splendid effect on the TONDA due to its high oleic acid content (65%) and also helps it release its antioxidents which act as natural preservatives: this filbert stays fresher and does not become rancid as quickly as other varieties.

Because cultivation is so limited, the TONDA is a delicacy reserved for a few local products, the most famous being the TORTA DI NOCCIOLE, or filbert cake, (p. 143) but it is also a refined accompaniment to aperatives and minced, may be sprinkled on TAJARIN (p. 81) or on meat. It is essential for such cookies as BRUTTI MA BUONI (p. 143) and is often addded to the luscious pudding BONET (p. 156). In Cortemilia and its environs one can buy bags of roasted filberts, pastry shops offer a variety of temptations using them and some bars have the TORTA by-the-slice, a highly recommended indulgence. But the NOCCIOLA was once known for more than its gastronomic qualities. For centuries, filbert trees were linked with the supernatural, viewed with fear and awe, for people believed this birch to be the preferred place for witches' midnight meetings and its great need for moisture made it a symbol for water diviners. During the Middle Ages it was thought that the ashes of filbert shells, mixed with oil and applied to a child's forehead turned dull grey eyes to black, though even then it was admitted that evidence for this was lacking, and that such ashes mixed with pork or bear fat would cure baldness, as could the nut's oil alone. Slightly more persuasive was the use of the oil as a remedy for arthritic pain. If these therapeutic efforts failed, however, NOCCIOLE could be enjoyed for their taste, described in the 1200's as being "sweet and pleasing to eat": they are the most easily digested of all nuts and doctors then suggested eating them roasted to stimulate the appetite and they were considered beneficial for the liver. Medieval documents show that tolls on Piedmont roads, especially to and from Genoa, were sometimes paid with filberts and the rest of the plant was also valuable: its leaves served for fodder, the nuts' shells for combustion and its bark is still used in carpentry.

Filbert Trees
near Cortemilia

Filbert Cake   Torta di Nocciole

7 oz. FLOUR
5 oz. shelled FILBERTS, minced
1 envelope YEAST
¼ cup MILK
1 TB. OLIVE OIL
3 EGGS
7 oz. SUGAR

4 oz. BUTTER, slightly softened
optional 1 TB. grated
LEMON RIND
8-9 inch baking pan, greased &
dusted with flour
Preheat oven to 350°

   1) Combine the FLOUR, NUTS, YEAST, MILK, OIL & a pinch
of SALT. Mix well & set aside.
   2) In a separate bowl, mix the BUTTER with the SUGAR 'til
creamy. Add the EGGS, one at a time, beating after each addition.
   3) Add the FLOUR mixture to the EGGS, a spoonful at a time,
stirring well after each addition. Mix in the optional LEMON
RIND, pour into the pan & bake 30-40 minutes. Let the TORTA cool
before slicing.
The TORTA is quite crumbly: some eat it with a spoon rather than a fork.

Ugly but Good   Brutti ma Buoni

5 EGG WHITES
14 oz. shelled FILBERTS,
minced
12 oz. SUGAR
pinch of CINNAMON
½ tsp. VANILLA extract
greased baking sheets

Preheat oven to 325°

   1) Beat the EGG
WHITES 'til they form stiff
peaks. Continue beating &
add the NUTS, SUGAR &
SPICES.

2) Transfer the mixture to a pot & over low
heat, stir 30-40 minutes with a wooden
spoon 'til the contents become "dry".
Drop by spoonfuls onto the baking
sheets: they should
be irregular in
form. Bake about
40 minutes. Let
the cookies cool be-
fore eating. They keep well in a
covered tin box.

In the past the TORTA DI
NOCCIOLE was made only for
very special occasions & normally did not contain flour:
any flour available was saved
to make bread & putting it
in the cake would have
seemed almost wasteful.

Chocolate and GIANDUIA are not the only reasons why the Piedmont is famous for its sweets: in cookbooks printed there in the 18th and 19th centuries the number of recipes for DOLCI is second only to those for meat. This abundance is sometimes explained by the fact that the chefs of Italy's royal family, some of whom had trained in France and thus were familiar with that country's tradition of pastries, were constantly trying to make new, enticing delicacies to delight the Savoys and impress their guests. To this day, Turin is famous for an incredible array of MIGNON, beautiful, dainty, bite-sized morsels that serious, mature adults enjoy with the gusto of children and, indeed, are more fun to eat than a piece of pie or cake with a fork. Among these sweets, cookies are prominent, perhaps the best known being SAVOIARDI, obviously named for the royal family; their English name, Ladyfingers, refers to their long slender form. They are used in numerous desserts, Piedmontese and not: pastry shops often sell their own, some people make them at home and thanks to industrial production, they are easily available.

These cookies were very likely born as cake, as far back as the 1300's, and served political as well as culinary purposes. In 1348, the young Amedeo VI (1334-1383), known as IL CONTE VERDE or the "Green Knight", -after winning a jousting tournament in Bourg-en-Bress in 1353 in which all the knights wore green, his clothes, furnishings, military banners etc. were always of this color- presented a huge confection of SAVOIARDI dough to the King of Bohemia, Charles IV of Luxembourg, his guest at the Savoys' principal estate in Chambery. Carried on a silver tray, it was a reproduction of that castle and its grounds, surrounded by snow-capped mountains and crowned with the emblem of Luxembourg and was inspired by Middle Eastern and Byzantine traditions of decorating sumptuously laid tables at banquets and wedding festivities with elaborate sculptures made of sugar mixed with gum arabic or almond paste. European rulers enthusiastically adopted this custom, modifying it to fit their particular needs and purposes.

Although these sweet creations appeared at the end of the meal, they were not desserts in the modern sense for this category of food was not yet born. After being introduced into Europe by the Arabs in the 8th century, sugar was used first as medicine, for making syrups to treat throat problems and coughs and then, as a spice. The cooks of the wealthy added this exotic, expensive ingredient to all sorts of dishes, including pasta, vegetables, meat, fish and fruit sherbets. While it seems that people, especially Italians, had a genuine passion for this taste, since it was a luxury, sugar was an admired and coveted status symbol revered for more than just its flavor. The sugar ornaments like that offered by Amedeo VI usually depicted architectural possessions, mythologial figures, ancient divinities or military victories and both their form and ingredients represented a host's power, wealth and generosity. Called TRIONFI, or triumphs, they were named after the spectacular processions of soldiers, their prisoners and the spoils they brought home that ancient Romans staged to celebrate their greatest conquests –to warrent a TRIONFO a commander's army had to slay at least 50,000 enemy soldiers- and their importance was more political than gastronomic. Protagonists of ostentacious banquets that were part theater and part pomp, they were made to impress and the anthropologist, Sidney W. Mintz, in his book "Sweetness and Power", suggests that in eating these sculptures guests recognized and reaffirmed their host's authority, a theory supported by the fact that Amadeo, who was but 14 years old when the presentation described above took place, not only greatly extended the Savoy's dominion in the Piedmont during his 40 year reign, taking control over numerous smaller and weaker feudal dynasties, but he was also the first Savoy to play a leading role in European political events. The sweet castle produced its desired effect on Charles IV: when he was crowned Holy Roman Emperor he raised Amedeo's title to Duke and made him his Imperial Representative.

Thanks to the growing skill of pastry cooks, during the 15 and 1600's the TRIONFI beame true works of art but they were to be replaced by a new creation. In 1710, Europe, or Meissen, Germany to be exact, finally discovered the secret of making hard Chinese porcelain and Italian production was soon underway: after Venice (1720), Florence (Doccia, 1735), and Naples (Capodimonte, 1737), a factory opened in Vinovo, near Turin, in 1776. In addition to decorative pieces, table settings, mirror frames, candle holders etc. elaborate TRIONFI were made. Kaolin, feldspar and quartz replaced the sugar and almonds and though these marvels could no longer be eaten, they had the advantage of being reusable. Similar objects were made of glass on the island of Murano, called both TRIONFI and DESSERI, recalling their historic and saccarine origins.

The use of food to evoke amazement, delight or reverence is common to all periods of history and thus it is not surprising that the cookbook by Giovanni Vialardi, head chef and ex-

Wafer Fort, engraving from "La cucina classica" by Urbano Dubois & Emilio Bernard, printed in Milan, 1877 (1ª. ed., Paris, 1856). As described in the text, the Fort & its hexogonal tower are of the natural color of the cooked pastry dough; the top of the round towers, door etc. are white almond paste, the waterfall is spun sugar. The arch has a wooden armature disguised with cookies.
Private Collection, Venice

pert pastry cook for the House of Savoy in the 1800's includes instructions for preparing complicated "compositions". These romanticized reconstructions of the famous Renaissance "triumphs" were meant to be made by dilettante cooks in the kitchens of the comfortable middle-class and thus were no longer symbols of military victories but, instead, of bourgeois well-being.

The TRIONFO of Chambery was a sort of sponge cake made of sugar, eggs and flour which during the following centuries was called GATTO' DI TORINO, GATTO' DI SAVOIA and GATTO' ALLA SAVOIARDA, Italianized forms of the French GATEAU DE SAVOIE, as it was called in the House of Savoy's original language. The recipe for it in the book "Il cuoco piemontese perfezionato a Parigi", published anonymously in Turin in 1766 and reprinted 22 times before 1850, calls for 14 eggs, their equal weight of sugar and half this weight of flour. The yolks and sugar are beaten by hand together for an hour, the stiffly whipped whites added and then, bit by bit, the flour —grated citron is optional. Baked 90 minutes, if it became a pleasing golden color it was eaten as it was but if it darkened, the author recommended covering it with white icing made from sugar, citron juice and egg white and eating it only once this dried.

This dough was also being used to make cookies as early as the mid-1600's, such as those in the magnificent edible TRIONFI prepared for the three banquets that the Duke of Mantua and Monferrato, Carlo II Gonzaga, offered in honor of Queen Christina of Sweden in 1655. Her intellectual interests had brought her in contact with leading philosophers and scientists and the devout Catholicism of one of these, Descartes, led her to convert to that religion and renounce her throne. On the way to Rome to receive communion from Pope Alexander VII, she stopped in Mantua: its Court was renowned for its lavish feasts and Carlo is most remembered for his squandering of money for processions and festivities. The menus for Christina's banquets were recorded by Bartolomeo Stefani, head chef for the Gonzagas and responsible for their Court's incomparable meals: in his book, "L'arte di cucinare bene" (the art of cooking well), printed in Mantua in 1662 and reprinted several times into the early 1700's, there is a recipe for BISCOTTINI ALLA SAVOIARDA, or little Savoy cookies.

According to Stefani, they were becoming quite popular and fashionable but as few cookbooks were printed in the 1700's in Italy, documentation is lacking. This growing fame is suggested, however, in Francesco Leonardi's "L'apicio moderno", published in Rome in the 1790's. He was head chef for the German-born Empress of Russia, Catherine the Great (1729-1796), and his book includes a recipe for a TORTA DI FAVOLE (fragole) ALLA NAPOLETANA, a strawberry cake from Naples that exploited what may be these cookies' greatest merit: because they absorb liquids and give body to creamy consistencies, they are often combined with fresh fruit and are essential for making such famous desserts as Bavarian Cream, charlottes, ZUPPA INGLESE and TIRAMISU'. Very similar to SAVOIARDI are BISCOTTI DI NOVARA; named for that city, they were born in the early 1800's and after 1850 recipes for them often appear with, or instead of, Ladyfingers and like them, are now industrially made.

Savoiardi

Preheat oven to 350°

4 EGGS, separated
3 ½ oz. SUGAR
3 oz. FLOUR & 1 oz. POTATO STARCH, sifted together
1 TB. POWDERED SUGAR
{**optional** a bit of grated LEMON or ORANGE RIND, added to the FLOUR mixture}
{**optional** pastry bag}
baking sheets or special SAVOIARDI tins, buttered & dusted with flour
tea strainer

1) Beat the EGG YOLKS with ¾ of the granulated SUGAR 'til frothy & almost white & add a pinch of SALT. Some historic recipes recommend beating for 30-60 minutes.

2) Add the FLOUR & STARCH in a slow, continuous stream, stirring constantly with a wooden spoon.

3) Beat the EGG WHITES 'til stiff & with a rubber spatula gently fold them into the FLOUR-SUGAR mixture, taking care they do not lose their airiness.

4) Drop spoonfuls of the batter onto the baking sheets in long, thin finger-like shapes or into the molds. If using a pastry bag, fill it with the batter & without a tip, squeeze onto the sheets or molds.

5) Combine the remaining SUGAR with the POWDERED SUGAR & pass half of this through a tea strainer onto the cookies. Let sit 10 minutes so the SUGAR is absorbed, repeat with the rest of the SUGAR & let sit 2-3 minutes.

6) Bake 20-25 minutes, 'til the cookies are slightly puffed & have taken on a very light golden color. Remove from baking sheet or mold & let cool on a rack.

SAVOIARDI keep well in a covered tin box.

Biscottini di Novara

Biscottini Di Novara, one of 20 tiny illustrations on the cover of "Il cuoco piemontese ad uso della Lombardia", printed in Milan in 1826. It is a "modern" adaptation of the anonymous book printed in Turin in 1766, written for the region of Lombardy. The other foods shown on the cover (the book measures 12.5 x 20 cm.) include mortadella of Bologna, MOSTARDA of Cremona, oil from Lucca, wine of the Piedmont, anchovies from Genoa, pigs' feet from Modena etc. Marciana Library, Venice

Biscottini di Novara

Amaretti   Almond Macaroons

AMARETTI, literally "little bitters", are almond macaroons, reputedly born sometime before 1750, when a certain Francesco Moriondo, a chef at the Savoy Court in Turin, combined finely ground sweet and bitter almonds with sugar and egg whites, formed this dough into tiny mounds and baked them. The results were positive and when he later moved to the town of Mombaruzzo in the Monferrato, he dedicated himself to making AMARETTI, an activity that continues there to this day and has brought international fame to this farming community. He was probably inspired by similar sweets from Sicily where cloistered nuns often made little cookies consisting of grated or crushed sweet almonds or pistachios, sugar and egg whites, recipes inherited from Arab cuisine. Like their counterparts in Italian convents, these women were famous for their pastries. Although originally meant to be symbolic gifts or offerings, these sweets were to become treats that wealthy lay people bought and thus were an important source of revenue and, according to some historians, they provided one of the few ways in which the nuns could express their creativity, facilitated by the fact that these closed, self-sufficient institutions normally had ovens which, 'til the 1800's, were a luxury reserved for rich people and professional bakers. It has been suggested that Moriondo's contribution was the addition of bitter almonds but it may be that he was the first to make AMARETTI "commercially". Notable AMARETTI are produced in other places in the Piedmont, and nearby Liguria, some with filberts instead of almonds but all sharing a pleasing, soft consistency, chewy and moist, and are used in making such traditional dishes as FRITTO MISTO (p.104-105), stuffed onions (p. 40-41), stuffed peaches (p. 149) and BONET (p. 156). Instead of bitter almonds, which are a bit toxic and not available in the United States (but in small doses, as in AMARETTI, are absolutely harmless) finely ground apricot pits may be used.

During the Middle Ages almonds were eaten as a remedy for anxiety & to prevent drunkeness; compresses of almond paste were applied to the temples to relieve headaches & induce drowsiness.

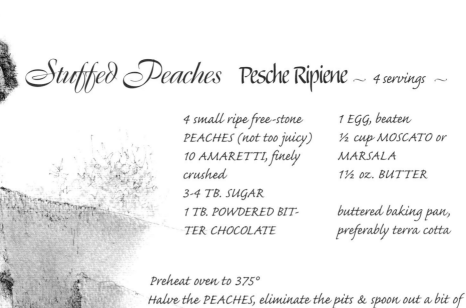

Abruzzo

Stuffed Peaches   Pesche Ripiene ~ 4 servings ~

4 small ripe free-stone
PEACHES (not too juicy)
10 AMARETTI, finely
crushed
3-4 TB. SUGAR
1 TB. POWDERED BIT-
TER CHOCOLATE

1 EGG, beaten
½ cup MOSCATO or
MARSALA
1½ oz. BUTTER

buttered baking pan,
preferably terra cotta

Preheat oven to 375°
Halve the PEACHES, eliminate the pits & spoon out a bit of
the pulp from the center. Chop the pulp with the
AMARETTI & add half the SUGAR, the CHOCOLATE, EGG
& WINE & mix well. Fill the PEACHES with the mixture,
rounding it on top. Arrange in the baking pan, sprinkle with
the remaining SUGAR & dot with bits of BUTTER. Bake 45-60
minutes. Serve tepid or at room temperature.

This dish is very popular during the summer when beautiful local
peaches fill the markets. While the cultivation of this fruit dates
back several centuries, it was only in the late 1800's that they began to be a specialized crop, raised in orchards. Before then,
PESCHE DI VIGNA were used, "vine peaches", called so because the
trees were planted between rows of grape vines. Before private homes
had ovens, women would bring their trays of prepared peaches to local bakers who
baked them in the heat remaining in their ovens after they finished making
bread. Both of these traditions have changed. It was verified that planting
crops among grape vines was detrimental for the grapes —and for wine-
for it prevented air from circulating & nowadays virtually all homes
have ovens.

Almond Macaroons
Amaretti

7 oz. SUGAR
4 oz. shelled, skinned
SWEET ALMONDS
3 oz. shelled, skinned
BITTER ALMONDS
2-3 EGG WHITES
POWDERED SUGAR
Baking sheets buttered
& dusted with flour
Pastry bag with plain nozzle

Amaretti from
Acqui
Terme

Pound the ALMONDS with a mortar & pestle to a
very fine consistency & blend in the SUGAR, a bit at
a time, continually pounding. Add the EGG WHITES,
gently working them into the mixture for about 10 minutes: the
dough should become firm but not hard, soft but not limp & hold its
shape if dropped from a spoon. Put the batter in the pastry bag &
squeeze out little mounds onto the baking sheet, about 2 inches apart.
Sprinkle with POWDERED SUGAR & let sit 2-3 hours: they will become wider & flatter. Preheat oven to 325° & bake 20-30 minutes.

149

Krumiri

KRUMIRI are a specialty of Casale Monferrato. There is something appealing in the fact that while in the past this city was famous for its military importance –until dismantled in 1680, it maintained one of Europe's best-equipped fortresses- its present renown is in part due to a cookie whose name and form both invite speculation. Created in the 1870's by a pastry cook, Domenico Rossi, who wanted to make something new for his friends, its name, KRUMIRO, is said to come from a liqueur popular at the time in the Piedmont and not from the nomadic Berber tribe of that name in Tunisia. Encouraged by his friends' enthusiastic response to this cookie, Rossi offered it to the public in 1878, as verified by advertisements for it that appeared in local newspapers. Its distinctive shape is thought to pay homage to the exuberant handlebar moustache of Italy's first King, Vittorio Emanuele II (1820-1878), and to the man himself, presenting a pleasing contrast between a courageous military figure, whose gruff manner and rather unkempt appearance belied an astute, sensitive intelligence, and the elegant, sinuous form of a fragrant cookie.

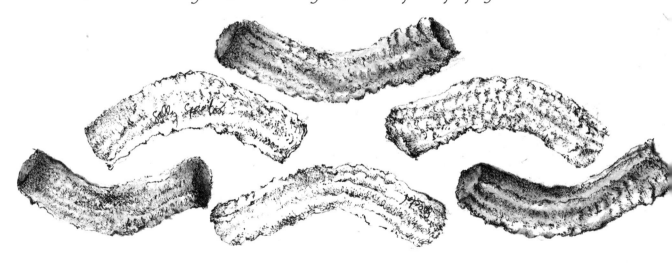

The proportions of the KRUMIRO'S relatively standard ingredients –corn and wheat flour, butter, sugar, egg yolks and vanilla- and the high temperature it is baked at produce a remarkable BISCOTTO: the heat gives them a dark golden-brown color and as it eliminates their moisture, they stay fresh for several weeks if kept in a closed tin. Their solid consistency makes them perfect for dunking, their crunchiness makes them satisfyingly chewy. These qualities were quickly recognized, for when presented in the Agricultural Pavillion at the World's Exposition held in Turin in 1884, they were highly praised and won a bronze medal. In 1885 Rossi obtained a patent for his recipe which continued to win prizes; its popularity led to imitations and industrial production, much inferior to the unique KRUMIRO still made in Casale.

When the mosquito netting around the infant Vittorio Emanuele's bed caught fire in 1822, his wet nurse lost her life to save his, an incident that led to rumors that he also died & the child of peasants was raised in his place. Royal or not, the person who became Italy's first King,' tho not inclined toward greatness, with common sense, courage, intuition & a sense of duty guided his country through difficult crises —both domestic & foreign- & negotiated events that completely changed its political character. Thus, while he much preferred hunting & mountain climbing,

he responded to the responsibilities & obligations his position imposed, the most significant being the unification of Italy, fulfilling a role not desired but accepted with commitment & seriousness.

Vittorio Emanuele II
(1820-1878)
1ᵗ King of Italy (1849-1878)
Engraving drawn by
A. Guadagnini, incised by
L. Paradisi
Royal Library, Turin

10 oz. finely ground CORN FLOUR
7 oz. WHEAT FLOUR
5½ oz. SUGAR
10 oz. BUTTER, cut in slivers
4 EGG YOLKS
{**optional** a drop of VANILLA extract or a bit of grated LEMON RIND can be added to the FLOUR}

Pastry bag with fluted nozzle
Baking sheets buttered & dusted with flour

1) Combine the two FLOURS with the SUGAR. Add the optional VANILLA or LEMON RIND. Work in the BUTTER with a wooden spoon & then, one by one, add the YOLKS, stirring well after each addition. Mix well to make a smooth, homogeneous dough, form it into a ball, wrap in waxed paper & let sit 60 minutes.

2) Divide the dough into 2 or 3 pieces, roll them into a sausage shape & put them into the pastry bag. Squeeze the dough onto the baking sheet in a continuous strip, cut this into pieces 7-8 cm. long & give each of these a gentle curved form. Bake 'til golden brown, about 20 minutes.

Bicciolani

Vercelli's contribution to the Piedmont's enticing array of cookies is the BICCIOLANO which is only made locally and thus is little known beyond its immediate area Its name presumably comes from the Latin bucellatum, a hard, usually round, cracker that kept for long periods of time making it an important food for ancient Roman soldiers and sailors: today, in some parts of Italy a BUCELLATO is a plump, ring-shaped cookie containing raisins, nuts and candied fruit. The BICCIOLANO, instead, is rectangular (about 3 x 1 ½ inches), not much higher than a cracker, dark brown and appears a bit plain, easily overshadowed by more eye-catching BISCOTTI. But, as is often the case in the Piedmont, looks are deceiving. In adition to flour, butter, sugar and egg yolks, they contain a pinch of ground nutmeg, mace, cloves, cinnamon, coriander, vanilla and white pepper, resulting in such a perfect blend of flavors that it is difficult to distinguish the individual spices: according to the Piedmontese-Italian dictionary by Sant'Albino (1859), grated lemon rind and fennel were also included. Pastry shops in and near Vercelli make BICCIOLANI: their size and texture may vary a bit but do not affect their delicate chewiness and at the same time, their seeming to melt in one's mouth. Teresa Flecchia, from Crescentino, just south of Vercelli, is credited with inventing them in 1803, but spicey, peppery sweet breads, a legacy of Arab cuisine, were common in the Middle Ages and Renaissance and BICCIOLANI most likely developed out of a long tradition of such aromatic, exotic delicacies.

Towers Of Vercelli
Tizzoni Tower, 15-17 cent., Tower of the An 14th cent., Vialardi T 13th cent.

1 LB. FLOUR
7 oz. SUGAR
1 tsp. ground CINNA-MON
a pinch of ground:
CLOVES, CORIANDER, MACE, NUTMEG, VANILLA, WHITE PEPPER
4 EGG YOLKS
13 oz. BUTTER, softened
pastry bag with fluted nozzle

1) Mix the FLOUR, SUGAR & SPICES together. With a wooden spoon stir in the yolks one by one, them work in the BUTTER to form a smooth dough. Cover with a cloth & let sit 5-6 hours.
2) Preheat oven to 375°. Fill a pastry bag with the dough & squeeze it onto a baking sheet in strips about 3 inches long or form a single strip & cut it into 3 inch pieces. Leave a bit of space around each cookie as they expand a bit in the oven. Bake about 10 minutes.

Introduced into Italy via Spain corn was to play a heroic role grain from the New World proved to be fun- ple well into the 20th POLENTA, or cessity. Ital- as animals here do, flour. Foreigners might be bread, but there is another flour which the Piedmontese, es- Cuneo, have raised to an art: from corn and wheat flour, sugar, eggs, MELIGA being one of several terms for corn in Italy instead of the official fore the advent of corn, MELIGA was for sorghum, or SORGO. The Italian from the Latin mel, is the origin of sweet pulp in the sorghum's stem. The tween SORGO and MAIS led to MELIGA PASTE DI MELIGA may be round, rectan- are found in pastry shops, bakeries and bars pily, since they have not

in the first half of the 1500's, in the history of food here for this damental in the diet of millions of peo- century. It was consumed mainly as corn meal mush, still very present but, for- tunately, now eaten more by choice than ne- ians do not eat corn in a kernel form, but instead, ground into meal or surprised at the scarcity of corn delicious way to use this pecially in the province of PASTE DI MELIGA are cookies made butter and commonly used word, MAIS. Be- the popular name word for honey, MIELE, MELIGA, called so for the physical resemblance be- being used for both of them. gular, crescent-shaped... and throughout the Region. Hap- attracted industrial produc- tion, they are for the most part ARTIGIANALI or homemade. A new appre- stone-grinding to produce the corn whose kernals are es-

"handcrafted", ciation of this simple, "rustic" cookie has led to a rebirth of optimum flour consistency and particular, local varieties of pecially suited to this method and render an unusually tasty flour are once again being cultivated in the Piedmont. This unostentacious sweet may look insignificant compared with other, more flashy pastries but it should not be ignored. Since it is so "common" it is often not very obviously displayed and thus it is recommended that one ask for it (recipe, p. 155).

Sorghum vulgare Pers. from Watercolor by Francesco
Peyroleri (1710-1780) from "Iconographia Taurinensis"
Library of Botanical Garden, University of Turin

Paste Di Meliga

7 oz. CORN FLOUR

7 oz. WHITE FLOUR

7 oz. SUGAR

5 EGGS

7 oz. BUTTER, slightly softened

{**optional** RIND of ½ LEMON, grated}

baking sheets buttered & dusted with flour

Preheat oven to 325°

Variations: CHESTNUT FLOUR & HONEY can replace some of the WHITE FLOUR & SUGAR

Combine the FLOUR, SUGAR, a pinch of SALT & optional RIND mix well. Form a "well" in the center, break the EGGS into it, add the BUTTER in tiny pieces & work to make a smooth creamy dough. If using a pastry bag, a bit at a time, put some dough in it & squeeze through a fluted nozzle onto baking sheet in desired shape (rectangle, circle, crescent...). Or, roll out the dough & cut into preferred form & put on sheet. Bake 10-12 minutes.

It is possible that this cookie found favor with the royal family since the Savoys' chef in the 1800's, Giovanni Vialardi, included a recipe for it in his cookbook that includes a pinch of ground cinnamon. There is also an almond-sized version, called MICHETTA DI MELIGA ALLA PIEMONTESE: MICHETTA is a northern Italian word for a small round bread roll & Vialardi adds that MELIGA cookies may be iced.

opposite page: "Iconographia Taurinensis" This unique work consists of 7,470 pages, all illustrated with watercolors of plants by leading Piedmontese botanical artists who overlapped with & followed each other over a period of 116 years, from 1752-1868. Begun by Francesco Peyroleri (2,000 illustrations), his main succesors were his nephew, Antonio Bottione (2,500 ill.), Antonio's daughter, Angela (1,000 ill.) & lastly, Maddalena Lisa Mussino (more than 2,000 ill.). All the plants were drawn from life; while Mussino's colors were made from mineral & vegetal components, her predecessors' were only from plants. No attempts were made to produce pretty pictures & the works are rigorously scientific but the great skill of these artists, especially Peyroleri, makes many of these pages strikingly beautiful as well as botanically significant. No similar undertaking compares with the "Iconographia": its completeness, continuity and quality of execution make it a monument of botanical art. It long served as a reference for both experts and students in this field; eventually replaced by mechanical reproductions such as engravings & lithographs, its value will never diminish.

The Botanical Garden is considered an Italian invention: the first ones were founded in the 1500's. Turin's dates from 1729, born, like others, as part of the city's university. It began with only shrubs & grassy plants & today includes traditional landscaped beds & green houses where some 600 species grow. An unusual feature of this ORTO BOTANICO is its "BOSCHETTO", or "little woods", covering 20,000 sq. mts.; some 100 species of trees have been growing there since the early 1800's & below it lies a meadow that has been left in its natural state.

Among the numerous notable botanists associated with this Garden, Carlo Allioni (1728-1804) deserves special mention. A famous medical doctor, renowned for his study of the pulse & arteries & versed in many of the natural sciences, was called the "Piedmontese Linneus" for his simplification & reorganization, for teaching purposes, of the classifications of the Swedish botanist, with whom he corresponded. As Director of the Garden he collaborated with Peyroleri on the "Iconographia" & on other fundamental works for the study of this Region's flora.

Torcetti

In many parts of the Piedmont one notices distinctive, delicate-looking cookies: sort of tear-shaped, light beige-almost transparent in color, the surface glistening with sugar crystals. They are TORCETTI, a name derived from the verb TORCERE, meaning to wrap, wind, curl or twist around oneself, which well describe their form. Since, like other BISCOTTI PIEMONTESI, they are local products, not factory-made, their precise shape & size vary from place to place. One of the most famous is that of Agliè, a town near Ivrea, which was the acknowledged choice of the Dukes of Genoa in the 1900's, 'tho cookies with this name were being dipped in hot chocolate in the 17 & 1800's. Vialardi's book has a recipe for them which, unlike today's, calls for eggs, milk, cinnamon & ground cloves.

1/8 oz. BREWER'S YEAST
1 LB. FLOUR
7 oz. BUTTER, slightly softened
SUGAR, for coating cookies
baking sheets buttered & dusted with flour

Dissolve the YEAST in a bit of tepid water. Combine the FLOUR with a pinch of SALT & mix in the YEAST. Add a bit of tepid water & work the dough 'til smooth & can be formed into a ball. Put it in a bowl, cover with a cloth & let rise in a warm place about 1 hour. Work in the BUTTER, kneading the dough 10-15 minutes 'til it is soft. Let sit, covered, 30-60 minutes. Preheat oven to 425°. Gently knead the dough 1-2 minutes. Roll it into pencil-like sticks. Dip them in SUGAR, cut into pieces 10 cm.long & form these into a loop or tear-shape, making sure that one end is pressed on top of the other. Arrange on baking sheets & bake 15-17 minutes.

TORCETTI keep for weeks in a covered tin box.

"Bonnet" Pudding

Bonèt ~ 4 – 6 servings ~

BONET is a Piedmontese pudding. Its name presumably derives from the metal mold it was traditionally baked in, which resembles a BERRETTO, a soft hat popular in the 1700's. Today BONET is often made in a loaf form. Many rstaurants offer it & it can also be found in GASTRONOMIE, or delicatessens, where it is sold by weight or in individual portions. Born in southern Piedmont, BONET is now eaten in many parts of the Region. Every family is said to have its own recipe. While there is little disagreement over its basic ingredients –milk, eggs, sugar, bitter chocolate & AMARETTI- & its being made in a carmellized mold, opinions differ over their proportions, if they are all mixed together or combined separately & then mixed & the importance of the optional rum. Thus, simple as this dessert is, it is amazingly varied: more or less sweet, more or less dense, it is consistently delicious.

Baking is preferred but BONET can also be cooked in a bain-marie over moderate heat. The water in the bain-marie should boil but never touch the pudding: this takes about 2 hours.

4 cups MILK
4 EGGS
7 oz. SUGAR
2-3 TB. powdered BITTER CHOCOLATE

7 oz. AMARETTI, crushed
optional 2 -3 TB. RUM

1 ½ QT. metal mold

Prepare the mold: Heat 2 -3 TB. SUGAR & 1-2 TB. WATER in a pot over moderate heat, swirling the mixture 'til the SUGAR dissolves without stirring. When its light gold color darkens to brown, pour into the mold, turning to coat the bottom & a bit of the sides. Preheat oven to 350°. Heat the MILK to almost boiling & let cool. Beat the EGGS, SUGAR & CHOCOLATE together 'til frothy. Slowly stir in the tepid MILK, the AMARETTI & optional RUM. Pour immediately into the carmelized mold & put in a pan of heated water: the water should come about 2/3 up the sides of the mold. Bake 40-60 minutes or 'til firm. When done, remove from the water, let cool & refrigerate about 6 hours. To serve, run a sharp knife around the pudding to separate it from the mold & turn onto a plate. It is usually eaten at room temperature.

Zabaione & Canestrelli

ZABAIONE consists of just egg yolks, sugar and slightly sweet wine –dry Marsala is often used but Moscato is preferable-, whipped together and warmed. Exquisite by itself it also fills and flavors countless other desserts. Legend has it that a cook of Carlo Emanuele I (1580-1630) invented this dish in an attempt to create something invigorating for the Duke's drooping health but another explation attributes its origins to a priest: in the confession booth women spoke of their husbands' flagging interest and he advised them to make a "potion" of these ingredients which would restore strength and relight passion. The birth of its name is also uncertain. Some say it derives from Pasquale Baylon, a 15th century Spanish Franciscan lay brother who supposedly followed Duke Emanuele Filiberto when he returned to Turin after being in Spain. Canonized in 1690 and revered as the patron saint of Turin's pastry cooks, San Baylon reputedly became SANBAJON and then, ZABAIONE or zabaglione. For etymologists, its roots may be in the Latin sàbaia, an ancient beer, or in the Old French CHAUD BOUILLON, a warm beverage, which became CIABUGLIONE.

Most recipes use one yolk, one tablespoon of sugar and half of an egg shell of wine per person. (a tablespoon can substitute for the half shell). A whole egg may be added to the ingredients which are all beaten together in a saucepan or the yolks and sugar may be whisked 'til they form frothy peaks, put in a bain-marie of boiling water and then the wine is added. The mixture is whipped constantly over low heat 'til it thickens a bit and becomes fluffy and pale yellow. It must not boil or be runny. Served in indivudual bowls or glasses, ZABAIONE is usually eaten tepid, accompanied by SAVOIARDI or TORCETTI, but it is also very good slightly chilled. As for its aphrodisiac powers, just eating it is already a sensual experience.

In the Biellese, ZABAIONE may be more liquidy than in other places and is often eaten with the CANESTRELLI of Biella and Cossatto. The word derives from CANESTRO, a wicker basket, and in terms of food, CANESTRELLI –little baskets- normally refers to very thin, light round wafers cooked between two studded hot iron plates, like a waffle iron. The patterns impressed on the batter recalled something woven, like a basket, which may explain their name. Such cookies have long been a traditional food for special occasions all over Italy, made to celebrate weddings, local festivals and holidays. This Biellese version is a relatively recent creation and even if one knows beforehand what these CANESTRELLI consist of, it is no preparation for actually eating them: a thin layer of chocolate between delicate wafers made from filberts. Once again, a sweet that may look ordinary but is incredibly, indescribably delicious.

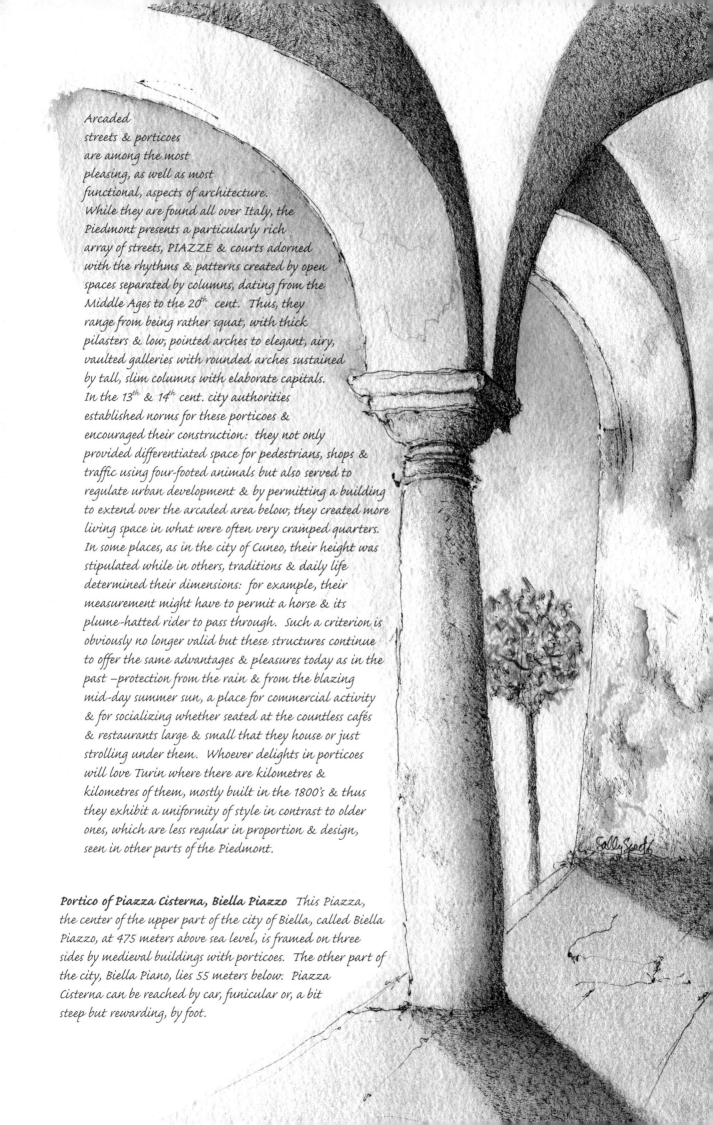

Arcaded
streets & porticoes
are among the most
pleasing, as well as most
functional, aspects of architecture.
While they are found all over Italy, the
Piedmont presents a particularly rich
array of streets, PIAZZE & courts adorned
with the rhythms & patterns created by open
spaces separated by columns, dating from the
Middle Ages to the 20th cent. Thus, they
range from being rather squat, with thick
pilasters & low, pointed arches to elegant, airy,
vaulted galleries with rounded arches sustained
by tall, slim columns with elaborate capitals.
In the 13th & 14th cent. city authorities
established norms for these porticoes &
encouraged their construction: they not only
provided differentiated space for pedestrians, shops &
traffic using four-footed animals but also served to
regulate urban development & by permitting a building
to extend over the arcaded area below, they created more
living space in what were often very cramped quarters.
In some places, as in the city of Cuneo, their height was
stipulated while in others, traditions & daily life
determined their dimensions: for example, their
measurement might have to permit a horse & its
plume-hatted rider to pass through. Such a criterion is
obviously no longer valid but these structures continue
to offer the same advantages & pleasures today as in the
past –protection from the rain & from the blazing
mid-day summer sun, a place for commercial activity
& for socializing whether seated at the countless cafés
& restaurants large & small that they house or just
strolling under them. Whoever delights in porticoes
will love Turin where there are kilometres &
kilometres of them, mostly built in the 1800's & thus
they exhibit a uniformity of style in contrast to older
ones, which are less regular in proportion & design,
seen in other parts of the Piedmont.

Portico of Piazza Cisterna, Biella Piazzo This Piazza,
the center of the upper part of the city of Biella, called Biella
Piazzo, at 475 meters above sea level, is framed on three
sides by medieval buildings with porticoes. The other part of
the city, Biella Piano, lies 55 meters below. Piazza
Cisterna can be reached by car, funicular or, a bit
steep but rewarding, by foot.

Wine   Vino

When and where grapes first appeared is not known: fossils of extinct species that grew some 55 million years ago have been found in Europe but the progenitor of the types cultivated today, the Vitis vinifera, was probably born about 600,000 years ago somewhere in the Eurasian area of the Mediterranean. Natural dissemination and crossbreeding, facilitated by the migrations of historic peoples, eventually produced many different varieties of grapes whose dark purple-blue or light green fruit ranges in shape from round to oval to oblong to teardrop and hangs in graceful bunches of tightly closed clusters to loose open ones.

Like many other fruits, grapes, or L'UVA, for in Italian the singular is commomly used, are consumed fresh, dried and as juice but it is their fermentation that has won them favor, fame and fortune. The wine that this produces has been drunk since the remote past and while, like the grape, the date and place of its birth remains a mystery, an Armenian legend attributes its discovery to Noah, of the ark. A sheep from his flock is said to have accidentally eaten fermented grapes and showed signs of drunkeness, both pleasant and not. Since Noah wished humanity to enjoy this same experience, when he was able to leave his ark after the flood, he supposedly planted grapes on Mt. Ararat. Similarly, according to the Old Testament, he was the first to cultivate grapes and make wine; having drunk to excess, he fell down in his tent, helpless "like a baby lamb", exposing his genitals which were respectfully covered by two of his sons, a subject often depicted by artists.

Wine making is actually thought to have begun about 2,000 B.C.: the ancient Egyptians, Sumerians,

Fragment of wall painting from Egyptian tomb, 2nd half XVIII Dynasty, **"Servant Decanting Wine with a Siphon"**, Egyptian Museum, Turin. In 1824 the Duke of Savoy Carlo Felice founded Europe's first great Egyptian museum, based mostly on the collection of Bernardino Drovetti (1776-1852), diplomat & military man from Barbania (Canavese). In 1824-5 the Frenchman J.F.Champollion studied these works which permitted him to verify his deciphering of the hieroglyphics of the Rosetta Stone. Greatly responsible for convincing the Savoys to buy Drovetti's collection was Count Carlo Fabrizio Vidua from Casale Monferrato, aware of the prestige that it would bring to Turin.

Phoenicians, Hebrews and Greeks drank it and in their religious rituals offered it to a Supreme Being. Grape cultivation in Italy, where climate permitted, dates back at least to 1500 B.C. and native Italic peoples, especially the Etruscans, were already making wine when the Greeks founded colonies in Sicily and in the southern part of the peninsula, the Magna Graecia, starting in the 6th century. Their arrival, however, would greatly enrich this activity, both culturally and economically.

The Greeks introduced the worship of Dionysus, god of wine, symbol of revelry and fertility and protector of the grape. His cult, probably born in Asia Minor, revered him as the representation of the natural forces of all living things and his followers expressed their devotion in orgiastic rites: female votaries, called maenads, or mad women, often wore masks with human faces during the most frenzied of these ceremonies from which Greek drama presumably derives. Dionysus' devotees were also known as BAKCHOI, the origin of his Roman name Baccus, BACCO in Italian. In an attempt to control the excessive behavior characteristic of these wild, licentious celebrations, the Roman Senate declared them illegal in 186 B.C. and Baccus was assimilated with another Latin deity, Liber-Pater, protector of fertility, god of virility, vegetation and liberty. Because wine was associated with sexual trangression and adultery, Roman women were prohibited from drinking it and to monitor their virtue, close relations had the right to kiss them on the lips so as to verify their obedience, a privilege that leaves much to the imagination. This law was tempered by the fact that sweet wine, which was not defined as wine, was permitted; bacchanalian subjects have been a favorite subject in Western Art for centuries.

The Greeks also exploited wine's potential profit. Prior to colonialization it had been produced on Italian soil only for local consumption but it soon became a valuable commodity of exchange. Wine making continued to increase and played a significant role in the economy of the Roman Empire, as seen in the emphasis the agrarian writer Columella (1ˢᵗ cent. A.D.) put on the financial benefits of planting L'UVA, discussed in terms of an invesment. Much of what he wrote about the techniques of viticulture of his day remained valid until the 1800's when machines began to replace manual labor.

Although soil and exposure are very important, climate, more than any other factor, determines a wine's quality: even the choicest grapes will produce mediocre wine when atmospheric conditions are wanting. Italy's particular position on the Mediterranean Sea is especially favorable for this crop -the   Greeks, in fact, called the peninsula Enotria, or "land of wine"- and the Pied- mont's topography adds to this already privi- leged situa- tion. Sur- rounded and pro- tected in great part by mountains that block cold north winds and crossed by numerous rivers and their canals, this Region's sun-basked hills, blessed with rich soil, are home to some of the world's best and most prestigious wines: the vines that produce them are the result of centuries of toil, ingenuity and experimentation. As the Roman Empire waned in the 5ᵗʰ century and Ger- manic tribes crossed over the Alps into northern Italy, most of the vineyards that had long flourished there were abandoned and the in- vaders' meat-butter-milk diet took precedence over the grain-oil-wine one of the Medi- terranean. That grapes did not completely disappear is seen in the Edict of the Lombard King Rothari, issued in 643, which lists severe penalties for stealing more than three bunches of them or the wooden stakes supporting the vines and breaking the vine shoots was also punishable, laws very pertinent to the area that would eventually be the Piedmont, for it had a decisive role within the Lombard Kingdom: situated on its western edge, it was responsible for controlling major mountain passes and communication routes, a function it fulfilled 'til not long ago. The earliest reference that specifies Piedmontese vineyards is from 754 and relates to selling wine in Vigliano d'Asti and was likely relevant for other places as well, for this liquid was of great importance. While it is sometimes said that most of the wine made at that time was reserved for rulers and feudal lords, historians remind us that until relatively recently, people had very little choice of beverages. Water was usually dirty and a risk to one's health: instead, wine, albeit often of low quality, was drunk by everyone and was a signifi- cant source of nourishment in the limited diet of the poor.

The farming initiatives of early medieval monasteries played a major part in the revival of wine making. Wine was essential for celebrating the Eucharist and it is said that it was the triumph of Christianity that gave a new impetus to the cultivation of grapes. In contrast, in the areas of the Mediterranean where the Muslim religion was adopted, this activity all but disappeared. With the rebirth of agriculture around the year 1000 vineyards were increasingly present in the secular as well as the ecclesiastic world and vines soon sprouted on hills and flat terrain in the Piedmont, as elsewhere in Italty. These grapevines were called ALTENI —alto means high, elevated- for they grew well above the ground on "live" supports, that is, trees, rather than low down, close to the ground as during Roman times. The deforestation that resulted from the return to farming as woods were eliminated to provide fields for planting meant that traditional wooden stakes, "dead" supports, were scarce and costly and trees were an economical alternative: in the Valle Maira, almond trees, no longer present, were used but almost any type would do, the most common being cherry, elm, maple, mulberry and willow. The vines climbed up their trunks and spread out along their branches and other crops, usually grains but also legumes and vegetables, were planted below.

The wine produced from these grapes was used for more than just liturgical purposes and drinking. Its alcohol content gave it antiseptic properties and mixed with herbs and spices it was an important component of the medicines that medieval monks and nuns were famous for, used to treat the sick cared for in their monastery infirmaries. Manuscripts and books from the 13th to 18th centuries

es, near Montiglio, nferrato

163

Paliotto, stone altar decoration, 13-14th cent. from Baptistry of St. Peter, also called the ROTONDA, 1st half of the 1200's, now in the Museum & Crypt of St. Anastasio, Asti

show it was also used in alchemy and the preparation of cosmetics and it became a valuable commodity in the expanding trade of the late Middle Ages. Increasingly in demand, its production was encouraged: around Asti, for example, landowners requested the farmers who rented their land to plant vines and by the mid-1200's this wine −Asti was then the Piedmont's most important city- was a sign of prestige, as it is to this day. In other cities authorities granted untilled land to those willing to grow grapes and in some places, whoever possessed vineyards was obliged to plant varying amounts of muscatel shoots, this wine being extremely popular in much of Italy during the Renaissance. Vineyards were becoming characteristic of the Region: today, for example, the words wine and Piedmont are almost synonyms.

This crop's importance is reflected in the many Piedmontese statues, especially of the 14th and 15th centuries, that protected, regulated and controlled its every aspect, from growing grapes to picking them, from making wine to drinking, transporting and trading it, and include detailed descriptions of crimes and penalties involving these activities. These norms refer to trellises in the courtyards of urban dwellings, to ALTENI in orchards, to extensive vines near churches... suggesting that L'UVA grew virtually everywhere. While it was generally unlawful to enter another's vineyard, in Ivrea doing so for the sole purpose of eating a few grapes, immediately, on the premises, was permitted. Far more serious was stealing bunches of them, with higher fines if this occurred at night but some leniency if the fruit was not ripe. Taking the wooden stakes supporting the vines was also illegal, as in Rothari's Edict, and due to the continuing shortage of this material, in the 1200's cities took action to safeguard existing forests. Animals were not only prohibited from entering vineyards, they were not even to go near them or graze close to them: fines differed for big animals (bovines, horses, asses, mules) and small ones (pigs, poultry). But, the worst crime was damaging and/or cutting another's vines, for which punishment ranged from a monetary fine to exile, to amputation of the hand, to the death penalty. In fact, one of the most devastating things an invading army could do was to cut an area's vineyards, as did the soldiers of Frederick I, better known as Barbarossa, when they attacked Alessandria in 1174: the city lost that year's vintage but resisted the seige. To defend this crop from lesser dan-

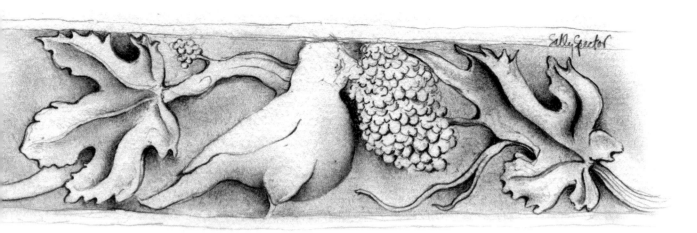

gers, communities provided themselves with official watchmen who were responsible for guarding the vines and enforcing the above cited decrees; called CAMPARI, they were chosen by local landowners and usually served for one year.

During the Renaissance the Piedmont's wines were much acclaimed. Ambassadors of the Venetian Republic referred to them, and the abundant vineyards they saw, in their RELAZIONI, or written accounts and in spite of limited transportation networks, they were increasingly exported —over the Alps to Switzerland, across the Channel to England and elsewhere in Italy. They were a prestigious gift given to important people: considered "instruments for diplomatic relations", archival documents show they were presented to royal courts throughout Europe. Among white wines, MOSCATO was the most appreciated, of the reds, GATTINARA and NEBBIOLO were better known than BARBERA, DOLCETTO and FREISA but it is difficult to be precise about which types were given for grapes and wines were not yet named and classified as today. The lack of a general system of organization was one of enology's biggest problems, a situation that would greatly benefit from the rational ideas and influence of the Enlightenment.

In the last quarter of the 1700's several treaties on viticulture were published in Turin, along with translations of agrarian and scientific works by foreigners of international fame. In some parts of Italy Agrarian Societies formed, the Piedmont's most famous one being Turin's SOCIETÀ AGRARIA founded in 1785. These organizations were dedicated to the progress and betterment of all aspects of agriculture, to promoting instruction and experimentation and to improving the health and diet of rural people. For centuries, attempts had been made to render food as tasty and appetizing as possible but the primary purpose of agriculture had always been to provide nourishment for survival: flavor, consistency, etc. were secondary, an option reserved for the well-off. But, the new ideas and attitudes introduced with the Enlightenment included a concept that would affect and improve alimentary products, which was "quality", that they could be better, even if this sometimes meant a reduction in quantity. With regard to wine, the Piedmont's close ties with France — geograpic, political and social- were very beneficial as that country was the first to apply scientific and technical developments to wine making. In the early 1800's, Frenchmen familiar with the Piedmont declared that this Region was capable of producing truly excellent wine for one "... could not desire better growing conditions than those offered by the hills there..." referring in particular to the exposure its hilly terrain makes possible.

However, in spite of this fortunate natural environment, the quality of the Piedmont's wines was decidedly mediocre: they deteriorated quickly and were drunk within one year, some becoming vinegar after only three months. While Roman amphoras had been sealed closed, to prevent contact with the air and to allow proper aging, this was not possible with the porous wooden casks that replaced them in the 5th century. Glass bottles would not be used for several hundred years; corks, introduced in England in the 1600's, for sherry, began to be adopted for wine starting in the 1700's and storing the latter in corked glass bottles became a sign of its being of high quality, reserved for a very limited amount of this liquid. It was much easier to have favorable atmospheric conditions and many historic stone-vaulted wine cellars are still used today but without adequate containers, this suggestive setting was, unfortunately, wasted.

By the 1800's, in the Piedmont, conferences, publications and itinerant libraries were responding to, and stimulating, interest in learning new wine making techniques. One of the most important of such initiatives was the Giornale Vinicolo Italiano (Italian Wine Newspaper) founded in 1865 by Ottavio Ottavi in Casale Monferrato which promoted new developments in farming such as spraying sulfur to combat the devastating effects of fungus, mold, parasites and insects on grapes: a terrible phylloxera epidemic in the 1840's that started in southern France and spread eastward destroyed grapes in the Piedmont, Lombardy and Tuscany and spraying was far more efficient than the maledictions and incantations of priests and altar boys used in the past. But, the greatest breakthrough came from research done by Louis Pasteur (1822-1895). Although for many people this French chemist's method for killing bacteria with heat, called pasteurization, is most associated with milk, it was discovered in 1865 as a result of his studying the dis-

Portable Instrument for Corking Bottles, Martini & Rossi Museum of the History of Enology, Pessione Chieri (Turin). The Museum is housed in the stone-vaulted wine cellars of the 18th cent. building where Martini & Rossi vermouth was first made. Corks revolutionized wine: they prevented bacteria in the air from entering bottles. Wine could age properly, becoming more pleasing, smooth-tasting, "softer".

eases that periodically ravaged L'UVA: heating wine for a few minutes prevented certain germs from developing which would otherwise alter its quality, thus adding an extremely fortuitous phase to the process of winemaking.

The first Enologic Congress met in Turin in 1875, its aims being to modify existing agricultural policies and to encourage the concept of specialization within the wine industry: farmers were to grow the grapes and sell them to competent professional wine makers. Separating these two activities made it possibe to produce better wine, with distinct characteristics, of more reliable qualtiy –apart from unforseen and uncontrollable factors, such as weather- and what had long been almost entirely consumed (90%) by the individual farmer-producers became a profitable commodity. But, these improvements were hindered by the Piedmont's plethora of different grapes and wines, a natural consequence of the fact that farmland was often divided into very small plots. In the mid-1800's, in the Monferrato, one square kilometer of land was farmed by as many as 35 different people and near Asti, many farmers had fewer than five acres. As for the grapes, a "census" of four provinces revealed that Alessandria had 130 varieties, Cuneo had 111, Novara had 130 and Turin had 200 and most farmers had no idea which types they grew. Virtually every town, city and province in the Piedmont had different varieties of grapes and a single wine was usually made from more than one of them. Attempts to bring order to this situation were thwarted by the fact that names were usually in local dialects and different places used varying terms for the same species. Cultivation techniques also received attention and an important "innovation" was a return to wooden stakes to support the vines. It was realized that grapes grown high on the ALTENI were inferior to those on the low FILARI, or wires, stretched between the stakes and this particular

Brenta, late 1800's, wooden container used for transporting wine: shoulder straps facilitated its resting on one's back. Considered a symbol of Piedmontese enology, it was also used in Lombardy, Emilia-Romagna & the Veneto. Its size varied from 49 liters in Turin, Ivrea & Susa to 74 in Acqui Terme & 84 in Tortona. Museum of Rural Life, Balbiano Vineyards, Andezeno (Turin), just east of Turin

change is held to be the principal contributing factor to improving the quality of wine. No longer shaded by the trees' leaves and branches, grapes received more sunlight; the crops previously planted between the ALTENI were eliminated, allowing air to circulate more freely and new methods for securing the vines' tendrils were introduced. These regularly spaced rows of horizontal vines sustained by slim, graceful, slightly irregular vertical wooden poles distinguish the land-scape in many parts of Italy today.

While all crops are visually pleasing, the curving, comb-like patterns that grapevines growing on hillsides create are certainly among the most aesthetically satisfying that agriculture offers us. Thus, considering that the Piedmont is 32% hills, and some of them quite steep —many in the Langhe are over 800 meters- and wine is one of this Region's major products with more than 90% of its vineyards on hilly terrain, it is not surprising that this landscape is not only beautiful but, if the adjective can be used for nature modified by human intervention, it is frequently also sublime.

This beauty is hard won, the result of almost

Vineyards Langhe, in the distance, Diano d'Alba

year-round attention and, 'til quite recently, much physical labor: it was calculated that one hectare (c. 2.4 acres) of vines required 150 days of work, compared to the 60 days necesary for the same area of wheat. At winter's end, which could be March in the Langhe and May in the Valle Susa, the soil was turned over to aereate and loosen it, a task now done by machines. Then, the vines were pruned to strengthen and invigorate them: so far no machine has been devised capable of executing this delicate operation. In the spring the soil was enriched with cow dung, now normally replaced by chemical fertilizers and the vines were, as they still are, tied to their supports with thin, flexible willow shoots or wire which, like the wooden stakes, had to be bought, making these the most costly part of growing grapes. As their leaves continually increase in size and number they must be removed for otherwise they hinder the grapes' ripening, jeopardizing their quality.

The harvest, or VENDEMMIA, was one of the major events in the calendar of rural life and its timing, officially established by local authorities, changed from year to year, determined not only by the weather but also by political circumstances: the threat of war or an attack of parasites meant an earlier than normal vintage. To prevent theft and sabotage among neighboring vineyards, all of the grapes in a single territory were picked at the same time, this being more difficult than it might seem and often done by women. They had to work fast, handling the bunches with great care, for if the skins were damaged precocious fermentation could start, and then the precious fruit was brought to where the wine making took place. The VENDEMMIA required great numbers of workers —sometimes an entire community was involved- and since time was of the essence, many aspects of daily life, both public and private, were interrupted. Various protective ordinances went into effect during the harvest: in addition to regulations already mentioned, it became unlawful to buy or sell grapes or even accept them as a gift. But, Piedmontese archives show that trangressions did occur.

Wine making depends on fermentation. Because the micro-organisms required for this to take place are on the grape's ex-

Tina, or wooden vat for treading grapes, woodcut from "Della eccellenza e diversità de i vini che nella montagna di Torino si fanno e del modo di farli" (the excellence & diversity of wines from the hills of Turin & how they are made) by Giovanni Battista Croce, printed in Turin, 1606. Croce, a Milanese goldsmith employed by the Dukes of Savoy also produced architectural works but is best remembered for his book on enologia, one of the first monographs published on the subject of wine. La Vigna Library, Vicenza

terior, its skin must be broken so they can come in contact with its juice, normally done by squashing it. For centuries, this picturesque phase of wine making, the PIGIATURA, was done by treading on the grapes with bare feet: this could be carried out in the wagons as the fruit was transported to where the wine was made but usually the grapes were transferred to a wooden vat specially made for this purpose. Motorized means, faster and more sanitary, have replaced this "primitive" method but there were advantages to using feet, for they can easily and spontaneously adjust and modify their force to provide the correct pressure and the must they produce is very soft, light and almost fluffy. Then, the

grapes, their skins and stems were pressed mechanically: examples of imposing and majestic manually operated historic wooden

Tina, engraving from "Le Vigneron Piémontais" (the Piedmontese wine maker) by the French agrarian Chevalier De Plaigne, printed in Turin, 1784. La Vigna Library, Vicenza

wine presses in the Piedmont's enologic museums confirm the fame of this Region's rural population's skill in carpentry.

Wine presses were expensive instruments, as verified by numerous archival documents: in the 1200's in Pinerolo, 18 trees pulled by 13 pairs of oxen were necessary to produce two presses made by several carpenters working 115 days. The investment was worth it, however, for the machine usually lasted more than 25 years and made it possible to execute as many as four pressings. Water was often added to the juice of the last cycle, which very likely also contained such residue as broken skins and stems: it was normally drunk by tenant farmers and manual laborers. This wine, very dark and said to be more thirst quenching and less conducive to drunkeness than that of the first pressings, was called VINACCIO, which today refers to cheap, inferior wine. But, no matter from which pressing it came, all of this wine was considered "old" after one year for it was not stored in air-tight containers. All of this has changed. Nowadays, virtually every aspect of wine making has been mechanized but, unlike the negative effects such methods often have on production, especially of alimentary products, experts agree that the quality of wine is now far better than ever before, a fact well proven by that of the Piedmont. While this Region is famous for its dry, full-bodied red wines, it is also home to Italy's most popular sparkling wine, SPUMANTI, from Asti.

In 1963 the DOC (DENOMINAZIONE DI ORIGINE CONTROLLATA) title was introduced to control and verify a wine's origin. It specifies which grapes are to be used for each type of wine, the maximum production permitted from a hectare of vines, the ratio of grapes to wine produced, the methods of wine making, the percentage of alcohol and the requisites for aging. Thus, the DOC mark guarantees a quality wine with characteristics particular to its natural environment. In the late 1970's the DOCG (DENOMINAZIONE DI ORIGINE CONTROLLATA GARANTITA) went into effect which subjects wine to certain analyses and to being tasted by a committee of experts; it is limited to wines already recognized as DOC for at least five years. The Piedmont boasts more than 50 DOC wines and some Barolo and Barbaresco ones have earned the DOCG distinction. While these initials provide authentic-ity and excellence, one should not be deterred from trying bottles labled simply VINO DA TAVOLA, or table wine, for many wine makers do not seek official recognition and prefer to rely on their reputation and the renown that personal dedication to quality has won them.

I hope that readers will forgive the brevity of this section on wine, a subject that for centuries has merited the attention of experts, connoisseurs and those who merely love it, to which I cannot hope to add. The fol-lowing pages are limited to mentioning the Piedmont's main grapes and the wines they produce.

Messengers Returning From Canaan Bringing Grapes, 16th cent. bas-relief.

Synagogue, Casale Monferrato, one of 13 synagogues in the Piedmont

Nebbiolo

One of the most important and prestigious of Italian grapes, Nebbiolo, called SPANNA in the province of Novara and in some places in the province of Vercelli, is responsible for some of this country's most famous, and best, wines for it is used not only for that of its own name: alone or combined with "sub-varieties", usually Michet, Lampia and Rosé, it produces such eminent wines as Barolo, Barbaresco, Gattinara, Ghemme, and Carema as well as, less known but equally DOC, Boca, Bramaterra, Donnaz, Fara, Lessona and Sizzano. Except for Donnaz, which comes from the Valle d'Aosta, all the others come from the provinces of Cuneo, Novara, Torino or Vercelli. It is no exaggeration to say that Nebbiolo is the "head" of the illustrious family of Italian grapes. It is somewhat demanding regarding growing conditions but its fundamentally robust nature has permitted it to adopt to a variety of terrain; though it grows in many parts of the Piedmont, and Lombardy, the area of the Langhe (Cuneo) is home to the most acclaimed of its offsprings.

Nebbiolo from "Ampelografia Italiana" published by the Ministry of Agriculture & Commerce, Turin, 1879. (from the Greek AMPLOS, vine & GRAFON, description) The formation of the COMITATO CENTRALE AMPLEOGRAFICO in 1872 was largely due to the efforts of Giuseppe Rovasenda (1824-1913) from Verzuolo (Saluzzo), internationally known expert on grapes & vine. His garden contained over 4,000 varieties of grapes from all over the world, considered the richest such collection in Europe. He established the basis for identifying & classifying them according to color, taste, form, leaves, provenance etc. The beautiful lithographs of the "Ampelografia" were done by various artists. La Vigna Library, Vicenza

The earliest references to it date back to the 1300's, one of them from the hand of the Bolognese Pietro de' Crescenzi: before retiring to devote himself to agriculture he served a few years as a jurist in Asti and described Nebbiolo as an "optimal" wine. By the 1600's it was called the "REGINA DELLE UVE NERE", or "Queen of the black grapes", as purple ones are called in Italy, and its fame continued to grow. Its intriguing name –NEBBIA means fog in Italian- is said to derive from the whitish, powdery aspect of its skin that makes these grapes, which hang in long tightly closed bunches, seem as if enveloped by a soft, grayish veil of fog. However, another explanation stems from the fact that since they ripen quite late, the fog typical of late fall weather is often present when they are harvested.

Many consider **Barolo**, made from Nebbiolo grapes, to be Italy's best red wine. Named for the town located virtually in the center of its limited zone of production, in the 1600's, to the already solid fame earned by its excellence, was added the renown that royal connections bring: a noble family donated land in the northwest part of this area to the Dukes of Savoy who then took a personal interest in this wine, producing it as well as making it more known. Of far greater significance for Barolo, however, was Camillo Cavour who, from 1832 to 1849 served as mayor of Grinzane, also within this zone. His concern for agrarian issues and dedication to agricultural progress meant that the land he owned there received particular attention and as part of his efforts to better the local vineyards, in 1840 he had the expert French enologist, Louis Odart, brought over from Reims. Odart's judgment was that, in spite of the extraordinary quality of the Nebbiolo grape, it would never make wine of equal quality if production methods were not improved and thanks to such changes, and to the introduction of new cultivation techniques, Barolo became a truly great wine. Cavour is also responsible for encouraging the bottling of wine. Previously, glass bottles had been used mostly like pitchers, for bringing wine from barrels to the table and not for storing it, but in 1850, after three years in wooden casks, he had his Barolo transferred to corked bottles to age, a practice that then spread to the rest of Italy. Barolo, made only from the sub-varieties Michel, Lampia and Rosé of the Nebbiolo grape, is aged a minimum of three years; after four years it is designatd RISERVA and when aged five or more years in wooden casks it becomes RISERVA SPECIALE.

References in medieval documents pertaining to objects used for pouring & drinking liquids, normally wine, are sometimes a bit ambiguous so it is not always clear which of these purposes they actually served. A list of the most common terms for pitchers & glasses in Piedmontese inventories & registers from the 14-16th cent. contains 35 words: 'tho it is difficult to ascertain their precise nature, these containers were very present in daily life.

Pitchers, glazed pottery, 1350-1400, from Moncalieri (Turin). Museum of Antiquity, Turin

The wine **Barbaresco** takes its name from a town in the area where it is produced, a limited zone lying just north of that of Barolo: like its neighbor, it is made exclusively from Michet, Lampia and Rosé types of the Nebbiolo grape and, not surprisingly, these two wines are often compared with each other. The history of Barbaresco is closely tied to the famous expert enologist, Domizio Cavazza, from Modena. After earning a degree in Agronomy in Milan he furthered his studies in France and upon returning to Italy in 1822 was named director of the newly opened School of Viticulture and Enology in Alba, a position he subsequently held in a similar institution in Conegliano, in the Veneto. In the 1890's he returned to the Piedmont and setled in Barbaresco, devoting himself to growing grapes and turning them into the local wine, activities that greatly contributed to improving its quality. Barbaresco is aged for at least two years; after four years it warrants the name RISERVA but it can continue to age for many more.

The town of **Gattinara**, which this wine is named after, traces its history back to the ancient Romans —the word Gattinara presumably derives from Catuli Ara (altar of Catulo) or from Catuli Area (field of Catulo) in reference to the victory of Quinto Lutazio Catulo over the Cimbrians in 101 B.C. in a battle fought nearby- but it was only in the Middle Ages that it began to be cited in documents. Its wine was praised in contracts of the 13th century relating to renting land with vineyards growing on it. During the Renaissance this wine was sent in small barrels to Rome, by sea from Savona; esteemed by eminent people, it was offered by Pope Clement VII to Charles V, King of Spain and the Duke of Savoy Emanuele Filiberto preferred it over other types. The Nebbiolo grape used to make Gattinara grows on the hills that rise between the Vercelli plain and the beginning of the Alps in the province of Biella. 'Tho it is the same one that produces Barolo wine, the terrain here is more stoney and dry than in the Langhe, the reddish soil more rich in minerals, thus creating a very different wine whose relatively high pH level renders it particularly excellent when aged at least four years, which warrents being RISERVA. A small amount of the local grape Bonarda may be added to the Nebbiolo one, sometimes called SPANNA in this area, which is used to produce two other DOC wines of this zone, Bramaterra and Lessona, often called Spanna di Lessona.

Barbera

Barbera, one of the most celebrated of the family of Piedmontese grapes, probably born in the Astigiano or in the Monferrato, adapts better than any other native Italian one to a range of terrain and climatic conditions and thus grows in many parts of the peninsula as seen in the numerous wines of this name from the north to the south of the country. The earliest references to Barbera wine go back to the 1500's and while it does not seem to have become widespread 'til the 1700's, since it was no doubt called by different names in different places, it was probably better known than historic documents suggest. The most famous Barbera wines come from the areas of Alba, Asti and the Monferrato: for the first two, only the Barbera grape is used, but those from the Monferrato may contain from 10-15% Freisa, Dolcetto or Grignolino grapes –a higher percentage would compromise its distinctive character.

L'UVA Barbera is used only for making wine and lends itself to producing both dry and AMABILE, or slightly sweet, the former being the more prestigious and better suited to aging which, after two years is designated SUPERIORE. The Asti, Alba and Monferrato Barberas have been recognized DOC; in spite of the proximity of these vineyards, their wines all have individual qualities, due to differences in soil, exposure and terrain as if, it has been said, each "speaks" the local dialect.

Dolcetto

Dolcetto,
lithograph from
"Ampelografia
Italiana",
Turin, 1879.
La Vigna Library,
Vicenza

wines are dry, with a slight characteristic hint of bitterness: it is the round blue-black grape that is very sweet and juicey and unlike the Region's other outstanding dark grapes, it is often eaten fresh. Since Dolcetto vines are demanding and sensitive regarding growing conditions, they are easily influenced by their environment: those grown just barely outside the most traditional area have their own very distinctive personality. There is one adjective, however, that is used to describe all Dolcetto wines: GRADEVOLE, or pleasing, agreeable: due to their low level of acidity they can be drunk quite young and after six months are ready to drink but a short period of aging can be very beneficial. The DOC Dolcetto wines are from the cities of Acqui Terme and Ovada in the province of Alessandria, from Asti, and in the province of Cuneo, from Alba, Diano d'Alba and the Langhe Monregalesi.

While this UVA PIEMONTESE is cultivated in the provinces of Alessandria, Asti, Cuneo and Turin –and it also grows in parts of neighboring Liguria- the wine produced from the vines on the hills in the Langhe, where it was probably first planted, is the most acclaimed Dolcetto. In spite of its name, DOLCE means sweet in Italian, these

Freisa

The **Freisa** grape, born in the Piedmont, has not spread beyond this Region and its cultivation is concentrated mostly in the areas around the cities of Chieri (near Turin) and Asti and the hills of the lower Langhe, around Alba, known as the COLLINE PIEMONTESI, or "Piedmont Hills". More resistent to disease than most other varieties, the round, black-blue-green grapes hanging in cylindrical bunches framed by three-lobed leaves produce a somewhat sharp tasting wine so in the past, it was preferred a bit sweet but modern winemaking techniques have made it possible to make an excellent dry one as well. Those of Chieri and Asti are designated DOC and after one year of aging both these wines are recognized SUPERIORE. The Freisa AMABILE is often a bit FRIZZANTE, more prickly to the tongue than actually fizzy or sparkling. Whether dry or sweet, these wines are made exclusively from the Freisa grape.

Freisa
lithograph from "Ampelografia Italiana", Turin, 1879. La Vigna Library, Vicenza

The **Grignolino** grape, born in the hills around Asti, was probably named for the numerous seeds it contains: in Piedmontese dialect GRIGNOLE means grape seeds, VINACCIOLI in Italian. Its cultivation, once widespread in the Region, is now much reduced for it is extremely vulnerable to parasitic infestation and inclement weather and even in the absence of such adverse conditions its yield is very irregular and usually quite low; moreover, it can be difficult to separate the fruit from its stem. The history of Grignolino, describd by botanists as an "interesting" grape, remains a mystery. Medieval records refer to a GRAGNOLATO or GRAGNIOLATO grape in the province of Alessandria, near Tortona and Casale Monferrato, used to make white wine but it has been suggested that it was also raised to make fizzy, light, dry red wines called CHIARETTI, very popular in the Piedmont during the Renaissance: whipped egg whites and salt were beaten with the wine 'til the mixture became light, or CHIARO. Today the Grignolino of Asti and of Monferrato Casalese are both DOC and may contain up to 10% Freisa grapes. When their grapes come from older vines, with a short period of aging these become SUPERIORI wines.

Recipes, Ingredients, Ect.

⊛

~ indicates recipe ~

Index of Places

Index of People

Selected Bibliography

Alberini, Massimo, Piemontesi a tavola, Milan, 1967.

Antolini, Piero e Guido Stecchi, Funghi e Tartufi della Provincia di Cuneo, Cuneo, 1986.

Baruzzi, Marina e Massimo Montanari, Porci e Porcari nel Medioevo: Paesaggio, economia, alimentazione, Bologna, 1981.

Berta, Pierstefano e Giusi Mainardi, Storia regionale della Vite e del Vino in Italia-Piemonte,

Accademia Italiana della Vite e del Vino, Milan, 1997.

Bevilacqua, Piero, ed., Storia dell'Agricoltura Italiana, Venice, 1989.

Bloom, Carole, All About Chocolate, New York, 1998.

Boneche, Il Piemonte Paese per Paese, Florence, 1993.

Bracco, Giuseppe, ed. Acque, Ruote e Mulini a Torino, Archivio Storico della Città di Torino, Turin, 1988.

Brero, Camillo, Arsetari dla cusin-a piemontèisa, Turin, 1997.

Capatti, Alberto e Massimo Montanari, La Cucina Italiana, storia di una cultura, Bari, 1999.

Cardini, Franco, Per una Storia a Tavola, Florence, 1994.

Cattaneo, Luigi, Il Caseificio o la Fabbricazione dei Formaggi, Milan, 1837.

Cibrario, Luigi, Storia di Torino, Turin, 1845-1846.

Comba, Rinaldo, Contadini, Signori e Mercanti nel Piemonte medievale, Rome-Bari, 1988.

Comba, Rinaldo ed., Vigne e Vini nel Piemonte medievale, Cuneo, 1990.

Comba, Rinaldo e F. Panero, eds., Il Seme l'aratro la messe, Cuneo, 1996.

Cornaglia, G., "Trasformazioni Agrario-Economiche dell'Astigiano nel Sec.XIII", Il Platano, Asti, 1981, pp.85-91.

Crestani, Diego, Anciuìe e caviè 'd la Val Mairo, Cuneo, 1999.

Consolo, Felice, *La Cucina del Piemonte*, Milan, 1964.

Dall'Oglio, Maria Attilia Fabbri, *I Sapori Perduti*, Rome, 1993.

Doglio, Sandro, *Gran Dizionario della Gastronomia del Piemonte*, San Giorgio di Montiglio, 1990.

Doglio, Sandro, *L'Inventore della Bagna Caoda*, San Giorgio di Montiglio.

Donna d'Oldenico, Giovanni, "La Ricerca in Piemonte di Zucchero da piante indigene durante l'occupazione

Francese", *Rivista di Storia dell'Agricoltura*, anno XXI, n.1, giugno 1981, pp. 5-16.

Faccioli, Emilio, ed. *Arte della Cucina in Italia: Libri di Ricette. . .dal XIV al XIX secolo*, Milan, 1966.

Famija Albeisa, *Grande Libro della Cucina Albese*, Alba, 1996.

GEC (Enrico Gianeri), *Gianduia, Famija Turineisa*, Turin, 1962.

Gibelli, Luciano, *Memorie di Cose: prima che scende il buio*, Ivrea, 1987.

Goria, Giovanni, *La Cucina del Piemonte*, Padua, 1990.

Gosetti della Salda, Anna, *Le Ricette regionali italiane*, Milan, 1967.

Gribaudi, Dino, *Regioni d'Italia-Piemonte*, Turin, 1966.

Lodi, Beppe e Luciano De Giacomi, *Nonna Genia*, Cuneo, 1999.

Messedaglia, Luigi, "Leggendo la Cronaca di frate Salimbene da Parma. Note per la storia della vita Economica e del costume nel secolo XIII", *Atti dell'Istituto Veneto di Scienze, Lettere ed Arti*, anno 1943-44, tomo CIII-Parte II, pp. 351-425.

Ministero Beni Culturali e Ambientali, *Le Cucine della Memoria: Vol.I, Piemonte...*, Rome, 1995.

Mintz, Sidney, *Sweetness and Power: The Place of Sugar in Modern History*, New York, 1985.

Montacchini, Franco, ed., *Erbari e Iconografia Botanica: storia delle collezioni dell'Orto Botanico Dell'Università di Torino*, Turin, 1986.

Montanari, Massimo, *L'Alimentazione Contadina nell'alto medioevo*, Naples, 1979.

Nada Patrone, Anna Maria, *Il Cibo del Ricco ed il Cibo del Povero*, Turin, 1981.

Nada Patrone, Anna Maria, *Il Medioevo in Piemonte*, Turin, 1986.

Nada Patrone, Anna Maria, & Gabriella Araldi, *Comuni e Signorie nell'Italia Settentrionale-Piemonte e Liguria*, Turin, 1986.

Naso, Irma, *La Cultura del Cibo: alimentazione, dietetica, cucina nel basso medioevo*, Turin, 1999.

Pradelli, Alessandro Molari, *La Cucina Piemontese*, Rome, 1998.

Prato, Giuseppe, *La Vita Economica in Piemonte a mezzo il secolo XVIII*, Turin, 1908.

Peyrot, Ada, *Dalle Alpi a Torino con Scrittori Stranieri del Passato*, Vicenza, (no date).

Picco, Leila, *Tra Filari e Botti, Storia economica del Vino in Piemonte dal XVI al XVIII secolo*, Turin, 1989.

Pini, Antonio Ivan, *Vite e Vino nel Medioevo*, Bologna, 1989.

Revelli, Nuto, *L'Anello Forte-La Donna: storie di vita contadina*, Turin, 1985.

Rangoni, Laura, *Le Vie dell'Acciuga. Storia, mito e tradizione culinaria*, Turin, 2001.

Segre, Luciano, *Agricoltura e Costruzione di un Sistema Idraulico nella Pianura Piemontese(1800-1880)*, Milan, 1983.

SLOW FOOD, Bra, Various articles and Pubblications.

Serventi, Silvano, ed., *Il Cuoco Piemontese Perfezionato a Parigi-Torino 1766*, Bra, 1995.

Watson, Katherine J., "Sugar Sculpture for Grand Ducal Weddings from the Giambologna Workshop", *Connoisseur*, Sept. 1978, pp.20-26.

White, Lynn Jr., *Medieval Technology and Social Change*, London, 1962.

Zangheri, Renato, *Agricoltura e Contadini nella Storia d'Italia*, Turin, 1974.

Dizionario Biografico degli Italiani, Istituto della Enciclopedia Italiana, Rome

Enciclopedia Agraria Italiana, Rome, 1952

Enciclopedia Italiana, Istituto della Enciclopedia Italiana, Rome

Touring Club Italiano, Guida Rossa for Piemonte and for Torino